the Citizen's Voice

the Citizen's Voice
Twentieth-Century Politics and Literature

Michael Keren

UNIVERSITY OF
CALGARY
PRESS

Published by the University of Calgary Press
2500 University Drive NW, Calgary, Alberta, Canada T2N 1N4
www.uofcpress.com

No part of this publication may be reproduced, stored in a retrieval system or transmitted, in any form or by any means, without the prior written consent of the publisher or a licence from The Canadian Copyright Licensing Agency (Access Copyright). For an Access Copyright licence, visit www.accesscopyright.ca or call toll free to 1-800-893-5777.

© 2003 Michael Keren
National Library of Canada Cataloguing in Publication

Keren, Michael
The citizen's voice : twentieth-century politics and literature / Michael Keren.

Includes bibliographical references and index.
ISBN 1-55238-113-7

1. Literature, Modern—20th century—History and criticism. 2. Politics and literature. I. Title.

PN3411.K47 2003   809'.93358   C2003-905790-9

We acknowledge the financial support of the Government of Canada through the Book Publishing Industry Development Program (BPIDP) for our publishing activities.

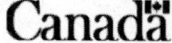 Canada Council for the Arts Conseil des Arts du Canada

Printed and bound in Canada by AGMV Marquis
∞ This book is printed on 100% post-consumer, acid-free paper

Cover design, page design and typesetting by Mieka West.

Contents

Introduction 1
We Are Not Immortal 15
A Bureaucratic Nightmare 35
In Quest of Authenticity 55
Resisting Big Brother 69
No Fire; No Smoke; No Rescue 89
Freedom and Responsibility 99
And History Continues 109
Being There 123
Death of the Novel? 137
Notes 151
Bibliography 159
Index 165

Introduction

In today's world, it is no longer surprising to find that people we "know" may not exist in reality. We know family members, friends and neighbors whom we have met, we know television celebrities, radio announcers and chatters on the Internet whom we have never met, and we also know characters created by novelists who become part of our consciousness even though they exist only in virtual reality. We love or hate them, wish to know them better or are afraid of them; we relate to them in a variety of ways and consider the political messages they convey to us.

This book analyzes political messages conveyed by eight literary characters: Hans Castorp, Joseph K., John the Savage, Winston Smith, Ralph, Meursault, Ida Ramundo, and Chauncey Gardiner. These eight are familiar to millions of readers around the world who have read the novels in which they are the main characters: Thomas Mann's *The Magic Mountain*, Franz Kafka's *The Trial*, Aldous Huxley's *Brave New World*, George Orwell's *1984*, William Golding's *Lord of the Flies*, Albert Camus' *The Stranger*, Elsa

Morante's *History*, and Jerzy Kosinski's *Being There*. They are also familiar to many who have not read the novels but have heard about them, seen movies based on them, read the reviews or have become accustomed to hearing expressions related to them such as "big brother" or "brave new world."

Obviously, these literary figures convey different messages to different people. Novels may be interpreted in many ways, and so may the political messages derived from them. The legitimacy of deriving political messages from novels may itself be challenged. I would like, however, to suggest a political theme that cuts across the eight novels and to argue that, taken together, they prescribe a model of political life. All eight characters studied here participate in the ideological, technological, and organizational processes of the modern industrial state. As they do so, however, they also reflect on their experiences, and by the very nature of their self-reflection, advance the notion of civil society on a global scale.

This is not an obvious contention. While literary heroes of the eighteenth and nineteenth centuries were assumed to convey positive political messages, twentieth-century characters were not. The heroes of the past were seen as engendering political organization and bureaucratization,[1] rationalizing specific social and political circumstances,[2] and providing the nation-state with a sense of direction by standing above its daily circumstances.[3] In the twentieth-century novel, the image of the hero has been shattered; its characters were seen at best as conveying negative messages on the breakdown of political norms and institutions.[4] An analysis of the eight novels from the perspective of the early twenty-first century, however, reveals a political message that has been largely overlooked, one promoting the notion of a global civil society and spelling out the features of the citizens comprising it.

"Civil society" refers to the plurality of individuals and associations operating within a state in relative autonomy from it. The autonomy is relative because as individuals and associations gain access to state resources they often bargain away some of their autonomy.[5] The term "civil society" is used to highlight the existence of such semi-autonomous associations in a state as well as to characterize states in which it is prevalent. In both meanings, it refers to a sphere of activity in which citizens do not act only as subjects of the state but think, talk, assemble, and act in matters that are of public importance, yet go beyond its imperatives. A state in which civil society flourishes may be contrasted to one in which government guidelines direct the entire sphere of human activity. This contrast is based on the age-old question of whether individuals are sinful, erring creatures in need of guidance or citizens capable of reasoned dialogue and action.[6]

The term "civil society," coined by Aristotle, was mainly used to describe civilized constitutional regimes.[7] It became a cornerstone in Hegel's political philosophy, representing a dimension of the state in which legal, professional, and ethical codes are observed. Hegel believed that civil activity, necessary to restrain both the individual and the government, could be conducted only in the state, which assures the necessary freedom from family, tribe, or church. But when the term was revived during the revolutions in Europe in the 1980s and 1990s, it was defined in partial opposition to the state. The aim of these revolutions, especially the struggle by the Solidarity movement in Poland, was to transform the state into a market economy. The intention, however, was not to replace one oppressive model by another, for the free market can also be oppressive, but to form a new notion of citizenship. In symposia held in the early nineties, the associations composing civil society were therefore conceived as balancing both the state and the free market. As Michael Walzer notes, civil society has no singularity of its own but complements other social forces; the members of civil society do not cease to be citizens of the state or producers and consumers in the free market. Once civil activity is assured, however, the state and market forces have greater difficulty in controlling the individual.[8]

This is where the power of "civil society" lies; the term reaffirms the long-neglected role of the citizen in public life: to retain self-consciousness and thus serve as a barrier against absolute control by hegemonic political and economic forces.

In *Jihad vs. McWorld*, Benjamin Barber calls for the introduction of civil society on a global scale. Global democracy, he writes, depends on a methodical internationalization of civil society. Viewing civil society as "a mediating third domain between the overgrown but increasingly ineffective state government and the metastasizing private market sectors,"[9] he speaks of the hope it holds for a democratic world:

> Civil society grounds democracy as a form of government in which not politicians and bureaucrats but an empowered people use legitimate force to put flesh on the bones of their liberties;

and in which liberty carries with it the obligations of social responsibility and citizenship as well as the rights of legal persons. Civil society offers us a single civic identity that, belonging neither to state bureaucrats nor private consumers but to citizens alone, recouples rights and responsibilities and allows us to take control of our governments and our markets. Civil society is the domain of citizens.[10]

In the international domain, where states are weak and markets dominant, civil society can offer an alternative identity to people who otherwise are only clients or consumers, or passive spectators of global trends they can do nothing to challenge. Barber offers a model of the citizen as an individual who has acquired a public voice. Although the model remains vague, Barber considers the character of the public voice as essential in defining the citizen and makes clear it is anything but the voice of "the divisive rant of talk radio or the staccato crossfire of pundit TV."[11] The media, he claims, have abandoned civil society for the greater profits of the private sector, where their public responsibilities no longer hobble their taste for commercial success.

There is a major difference between the individual presented in the media and the citizen operating within voluntary associations and non-governmental organizations. The two spheres are of course interchangeable but the notion of the citizen must be differentiated from the image of the sovereign individual promoted in talk shows, investigative reports, confessional TV, and the like. As Mark Kingwell argues in *The World We Want*, the media appear to respect people's identities in an absolute manner, a tendency that stands in contrast to their consideration as part of a larger community of human rights:

> If an identity cannot be challenged by reference to some larger shared goals, then neither can the preferences and desires that proceed from it. Thus, in a twisted way, we arrive at the toxic forms of narcissism, complaint, and self-justification that pass for individualism today: not just the rock-'em, sock-'em talk shows, in which people act out of their pathetic conflicts under Jerry Springer's cynically moralizing eye, but also the high-toned literary

memoirs and confessions that are the functional equivalents for people with more money and education.[12]

The mass media may have vulgarized the notion of the citizen but literature has kept it alive. Citizens whose self-consciousness is not shaped by entertainers and who combine a consideration for autonomy and community do not flourish on radio talk shows and pundit TV, but their voice has never been shut up entirely. The voice of citizens can be heard despite the presence of gigantic forces – including the mass media – mobilizing, overwhelming, suppressing, and despising them. When individuals were subjected to the structures and processes of the modern industrial state in the twentieth century, they confronted them in their private spheres, and a handful of novels made private concerns public. Thus, the "domain of citizens" was maintained even at times when the citizen did not seem to have a chance.

Ideology, technology, and organization played a central role in the history of the twentieth century: the world wars, the rise and fall of totalitarianism, the Holocaust, the atomic bomb, de-colonization, the Cold War, globalization, and so forth. National leaders, military commanders, corporation executives, managers, bureaucrats, scientists, and other makers of history spoke a language that showed admiration for the modern industrial state and helped advance it. However varied the visions of Max Weber, Vladimir Illich Lenin, Frederick Winslow Taylor, John Kenneth Galbraith, or Lee Iacocca, they all shared a belief in the capacity to mobilize people for the construction of a progressive future. But the people knew better. Not that the Bolshevik revolution, the fascist parades, the Allies' victories, the Third World awakening, or the space program did not generate great enthusiasm, but as the social-industrial structures of the twentieth century were constructed, destroyed, and reconstructed, individuals, in their private sphere, knew they were both the beneficiaries and victims of these structures, and this knowledge was articulated in a handful of novels promoting a modified version of community.

True, many twentieth-century writers were "fellow travelers"[13] of the century's grand ideologies, especially communism, but civil society also had its advocates. The novelist who, from a private perspective, exposes the modern industrial state's failure to fulfill its ambitious promises, and notes the price paid by the individuals comprising it, contributes to the development of civil consciousness. A special role was played by novelists, poets, playwrights, and other persons of letters who contributed to the collapse of totalitarian regimes. These regimes' loud promise of a messianic future, that is, a glorious future devoid of the evils of history and the troubles of politics-as-usual, could not overcome individual skepticism, as expressed, for instance, in Alexander Solzhenitzyn's *One Day in the Life of Ivan Denisovich*, or in Milan Kundera's *The Joke*.

In a study titled *Civility and Subversion*, Jeffry Goldfarb shows how writers, artists, and other intellectuals contributed to the breakdown of Eastern European totalitarianism by pursuing a free public life as an end in itself, within their own limited social circles. Intellectual activity constituted a limited free public domain within a totalitarian context, which was used to overthrow the communist powers. The author outlines the wider concerns this experience points to:

> It points to the desirability of an aesthetic position that involves an appreciation of the distinctive contributions the art of the novel (and of the other arts) has to make in enriching our reflections on the human condition.[14]

This point has been elaborated on by Christopher Hitchens in discussing the fall of communism in Czechoslovakia. The mighty occupation-regime installed by the full weight of *panzerkommunismus*, he writes, collapsed amid laughter and ignominy, without the loss of a single life, "as a consequence of a civil opposition led by satirical playwrights, ironic essayists, Bohemian jazz-players and rock musicians, and subversive poets."[15] Hitchens does not overlook the power of Soviet tanks but has this to say about it:

> The sword, as we have reason to know, is often mightier than the pen. However, there are things that pen can do, and swords cannot. And every tank, as Brecht said, has a crucial flaw. Its driver. Suppose that driver has read something good lately, or has a decent song or poem in his head....[16]

Milan Kundera, the Czech exile, articulated the role of the novel in enriching our reflections on the human condition. The spirit of an age, he said in a speech, cannot be judged exclusively by its ideas, its theoretical concepts, without considering its art, and particularly the novel:

> The nineteenth century invented the locomotive, and Hegel was convinced he had grasped the very spirit of universal history. But Flaubert discovered stupidity. I daresay that is the greatest discovery of a century so proud of its scientific thought.[17]

Kundera defines "stupidity" not as ignorance but as the failure of self-reflection – an inseparable dimension of human existence – upon the progress of science, technology, and modernity. Following this line of thought, it may be said that if the nineteenth-century novel discovered "stupidity," the twentieth-century novel reveals the danger once it is institutionalized in all spheres of human life. The eight novels discussed here take us through the twentieth-century project while reflecting on some of its most profound features, and as they do so they promote a model of civil society.

The eight novels are not "representative"; no equity based on race, ethnicity, or gender has been aimed at. Some countries, mainly European ones, are represented while others are not, some of the novelists are Nobel prize laureates while others are not, some novels are not necessarily the best written by these writers, and other novels contributing to civil society theory could undoubtedly be added. But the choice of these novels is not arbitrary; they include some of the best-known "political novels" of the twentieth century. Irving Howe defines the political novel as one "in which political ideas play a dominant role or in which the political milieu is the dominant."[18] The eight novels are "political" in this narrow sense: they deal explicitly with political variables such as ideologies, political parties, state–society relations, election campaigns, etc.

This narrow definition of the political novels locates this study in a middle-of-the-road position between an approach to novels as multifaceted texts that cannot be reduced to a political dimension but should be handled within literary paradigms and an approach to novels as political texts in their entirety whose role in a larger political discourse ought to be reconstructed. This study is also located between those who view novelists as determined by political circumstances and those who view them as free souls. Paul Cantor characterizes contemporary literary criticism by a strong historicist trend consisting of a devotion to showing how authors are formed by their social circumstances. "Study after study attempts to demonstrate how authors reflect and embody the prejudices of race, class, and gender they inherit from their society, only occasionally granting them a small role in helping in turn to shape their prejudices."[19] He contrasts this historicism to the classical approach in political philosophy, according to which human thought and expression are free of all constraints, material or otherwise. Cantor proposes a middle-of-the-road approach in which one distinguishes between the majority of authors, who are in fact bound by the horizons of the regimes under which they live, and those exceptional few who can see beyond the limits of their communities.

This study focuses on novels by the exceptional few who, while living in the complex global regime formed by the ideologies, technologies, and organizational practices of the twentieth century, transcend them by the power of self-reflection. Each of the novels exposes the private sphere of individuals as they struggle with, or adjust to, the ideological, technological, and organizational processes constraining their environment. Mann's Hans Castorp, Kafka's Joseph K., Huxley's John the Savage, Orwell's Winston Smith, Golding's Ralph, Morante's Ida Ramundo, Camus's Meursault, and Kosinski's Chauncey Gardiner are all characters rooted in twentieth-century reality, yet they are neither heroes nor villains. Most of them are defeated, but it is not necessarily their defeat that distinguishes them; they are not even "anti-heroes." They do not represent an alternative to the systems they live in (they are mostly members in good standing in society, the state bureaucracy, and the production process), nor do they represent the sense of mission found in national literature, or the human purity found in romantic literature. They are part and parcel of twentieth-century history and thus allow us to learn about the private sphere of its makers and victims.

The political analysis of the novels leads us through some of the major changes the world went through in the twentieth century. In that century, the human race, as Thomas Mann shows, played God in the form of daring scientific ventures conducted in thousands of "witches' kitchens," in which the delicate balance between life and death was upset. Scientific discoveries were made which gave us powers we didn't know how to use and technological inventions transforming our habitat into what Huxley calls a "brave new world." We applied the rational methods guiding scientific inquiry to human behavior without reaching prior agreement on who should be in control of the process. We tried to make the production process more rational and ended up with bureaucratic monsters turning life, as Kafka illustrates, into a nightmare.

Politics, the set of means by which we negotiate our existence with each other, was inspired by irresponsible ideologies. These ideologies, and the political parties representing them, became so strong that leaders, as Orwell demonstrates, believed they could overcome the laws of nature on the road to a new civilization based on fear, hatred, and cruelty. The great achievements in science, philosophy, and the arts were discarded by societies preferring the warmth of the organic community whose urge to hunt pigs, as Golding makes clear, is stronger than its survival instinct. Pragmatism and common sense were replaced by messianic yearnings propagated, as Elsa Morante states, by simple hooligans. Nazism took over, and terrible crimes against humanity were committed, but when Nazism was defeated we found ourselves, like Camus's characters, unable to allocate the responsibility for these crimes. We surrounded ourselves, and still do, with systems of communication sending millions of signals that threaten our mental health and change the way we live, relate to each other, and conduct our politics. Virtual politics, whose features were drawn by Jerzy Kosinski, becomes commonplace.

And yet individuals have not given up on self-reflection. The eight novels expose the private world of eight characters shaken by powerful forces and highlight the attributes of the citizen attempting to survive in some state of civility under these circumstances. "Civility" is the virtue associated with civil society, i.e., the assertion of one's autonomy as well as its willing restraint as a means to allow others to assert theirs. To quote Kingwell again:

> Together, in a general conversation governed by civility and restraint, we make and hear the claims of which society is composed. Together, then, listening and responding, we forge a fragile social identity. We come to reflect one another as part of the general interpretive project we call social life, and in so doing attempt to create the political order that will serve to hear and answer the various claims we will wish to put in play.[20]

The eight novels shed light on that political order and the virtues underlying it. Their main characters are analyzed as building blocks of a prescriptive model of civil society, whose incumbents possess the following qualities associated with each character:

1. The realization that humans are mortal, and that no scientific discovery can turn them into their own creators (Hans Castorp).
2. The understanding that interaction between individuals cannot be replaced by anonymous structures (Joseph K.).
3. The urge to maintain a sphere of authenticity within the surrounding systems (John the Savage).
4. The adherence to historical memory as a way to resist hegemonic controls (Winston Smith).
5. The reliance on reason as a means of surviving on the planet (Ralph).
6. The acceptance of responsibility despite the scant control one has over events (Meursault).
7. The acknowledgment that history cannot be transcended (Ida Ramundo).
8. The refusal to give up on the chance to change, develop, and fail (Chauncey Gardiner).

The citizens emerging from these novels are individuals aware of their weaknesses. They are mortal. They live in history and do not transcend it. Nor do they follow promises for easy redemption. They know they are doomed to fail frequently, but they are also possessed with an urge to survive and with the realization that survival depends on their capacity to interact rather than to destroy each other. That interaction takes place within social-industrial systems over which they have limited control. But as they take responsibility for the occurrences around them, and for their own survival, they engage in a search for real, not virtual, solutions to problems and construct a private space where their own autonomy and authenticity can be maintained as well as that of others.

The derivation of such a far-reaching prescriptive model from novels is not obvious, as political theorists have traditionally been ambivalent toward literary texts. Political theory is a field of study in which normative justifications of political life are formulated. Its origins can be traced to the claim, attributed in Plato's *Republic* of the fourth century BC to a restless sophist named Thrasymachus, that justice is nothing other than the advantage of the stronger. Political theorists have engaged ever since in a hard and desperate effort to respond to this challenge by formulating normative designs that would justify the state, and citizens' obligation to it, in terms exceeding the advantage of the stronger. The effort began with Plato, who proposed a model of the just state to be constructed by human reason. Reason had to remain free of the emotions sparked by mythological texts, which led Plato to demand that such texts be censored:

> Indeed, if we want the guardians of our city to think that it's shameful to be easily provoked into hating one another, we mustn't allow any stories about gods warring, fighting, or plotting against one another, for they aren't true. The battles of gods and giants, and all the various stories of the gods hating their families or friends, should neither be told nor even woven in embroideries. If we're to persuade our people that no citizen has ever hated another and that it's impious to do so, then that's what should be told to children from the beginning by old men and women; and as these children grow older, poets should be compelled to tell them the same sort of thing. We won't admit stories into our city – whether allegorical or not – about Hera being chained by her son, nor about Hephaestus being hurled from heaven by his father when he tried to help his mother, who was being beaten, nor about the battle of the gods in Homer.[21]

While advocating the censorship of literature, Plato himself used literary forms such as dialogues and fables to advance his ideas. Such ambivalence toward literature has always characterized the search for the just state to the extent that political theorists, although enriched by literature, developed a specialized jargon that excluded it. This exclusion was consistent with the specialization of the humanities and social sciences in the twentieth century, but has also been rejected by scholars, such as Paul Dolan, who realized the power of literature in generating political ideas:

> A large segment of modern consciousness is embodied in political structures; these, in turn, shape and are shaped by that consciousness. So politics cannot be understood only as the political scientist, the historian, the economist, the sociologist, the psychologist, or even the philosopher understands it. The novel provides its special kind of knowledge because it deals with the conscious and unconscious experience of politics as a human, moral, psychological and aesthetic phenomenon.[22]

In a symposium on literature and the political imagination held at York University, John Horton and Andrea Baumeister complained about "the abstract, decontextualised and ahistorical character of much contemporary political philosophy."[23] They claim that problems discussed by political theorists are posed in a form that makes them look timeless, hence the solutions will also need to be timeless. Political issues, however, are in some significant part about a particular time and place, which gives an advantage to novels and plays over theories striving at universal validity:

> It is in developing a richer, more nuanced and realistic understanding of political deliberation that imaginative literature may have an especially valuable role to play. Novels and plays, for example, seem much better at exhibiting the complexities of political experience and the open-textured and necessarily incomplete character of real political arguments.[24]

There are, of course, limitations to the reading of novels as political theory. As Horton notes, fictional narratives typically employ a vast array of literary devices and techniques, such as metaphor, allegory, symbolism, imagery, allusion, ambiguity, irony, etc., which make novels resistant to straightforward incorporation within other discursive contexts.[25] Susan Mendus argues that literary narratives often close theoretical options that political theory is concerned with because the authority of the text imposes on the reader an understanding of what the moral or political problem is, and a largely shared interpretation of examples that permit only those moral disagreements for which there is a textual warrant.[26]

These limitations, however, should not preclude an exploration of novels for the political ideas they convey. Every novel analyzed here addresses major normative political questions, perhaps the most important ones raised in the twentieth century. The following analysis is a political theorist's exploration of these questions in an attempt to understand the virtues of the citizen emerging in the novels. It is by no means an attempt to compete with the vast, rich literary criticism of these novels, nor is it an attempt to compete with the insights derived from positivist approaches to politics.

In an article asking "Why Political Scientists Want to Study Literature," Catherine Zuckert mentions the prominence of positivism in contemporary political science. In an effort to make the study of politics scientific, she writes, researchers in the 1960s sought quantifiable data and did studies that could be replicated. Unfortunately for the behavioralists, however, the major political events of the decade, including the civil rights movement and the war in Vietnam, could not be studied solely in quantitative or positivistic terms as the events were singular and the issues they raised obviously included questions of principle or value. Therefore, Zuckert maintains, a more democratic and pluralistic political science emerged allowing political scientists to look at works of art in order to study the aspects of human life that are most difficult, if not impossible, to study externally or objectively – the attitudes, emotions, and opinions that shape and are shaped by people's political circumstances.[27]

In what follows, I take advantage of this democratic pluralism and look at the political messages conveyed by eight literary characters in search of civility. I then argue that recent announcements of the death of the novel in the age of mass media may have been premature.

We Are Not Immortal

Paul Johnson's *A History of the Modern World* begins its tale of the twentieth century on May 29, 1919, when photographs of a solar eclipse, taken on an island off West Africa and in Brazil, corroborated Einstein's special theory of relativity. This is indeed a good starting point because the theory of relativity symbolizes, mainly as a result of the mix-up between "relativity" and "relativism," the fading hope for a world comprehended by common sense. Just as the linearity of space was challenged by Einstein, so were social, economic, and political truisms, e.g., the assumption, held by foreign ministries in the nineteenth century that the international system operates in accordance with Newtonian rules assuring a "balance of power."

Johnson shows how the falsification of physical theorems considered absolute for two hundred years, accompanied by Freud's contention that human beings are irrational and the Marxist belief in economic determinism, led to confusion:

Marx, Freud, Einstein all conveyed the same message to the 1920s: the world was not what it seemed. The senses, whose empirical perceptions shaped our ideas of time and distance, right and wrong, law and justice, and the nature of man's behavior in society, were not to be trusted. Moreover, Marxist and Freudian analysis combined to undermine, in their different ways, the highly developed sense of personal responsibility, and of duty towards a settled and objectively true moral code, which was at the centre of nineteenth century European civilization.[1]

These cultural uncertainties, as well as the political uncertainty of the early twentieth century caused by colonial expeditions that disturbed the European peace, led to the angst described in many writings of the era. In his autobiography, Stephan Zweig shows how his life, as a person born into nineteenth-century European civilization with its stable class system and fixed moral codes, was affected:

> We, who have been hounded through all the rapids of life, we who have been torn loose from all roots that held us, we, always beginning anew when we have been driven to the end, we, victims and yet willing servants of unknown, mystic forces, we, for whom comfort has become a saga and security a childhood dream, we have felt the tension from pole to pole and the eternal dread of the eternal new in every fibre of our being.[2]

Nobody expresses that "eternal dread of the eternal new" more forcefully than Thomas Mann in *The Magic Mountain*. Mann was seen as "a seismograph, delicately measuring the quaking earth of his century."[3] As Michael Harrington notes:

> Mann is the most relevant to a study of the contemporary decadence. He lived through all the unnerving transitions of the period: the turn of the century, World War I, the stultification of the German middle class, the rise of fascism, World War II, and the Cold War. Not only did he write of these incredible times; the times wrote his life as if it were one of his novels. In

his tempestuous fusion of autobiography and art, the inability of a culture to understand its own revolution becomes personal and evocative.[4]

Thomas Mann was born in the German town of Lübeck in 1875. His father, a senator in the local government, died in 1890, and shortly afterwards the family moved to Munich, where Thomas worked as an unpaid apprentice clerk in a fire insurance company. His first short stories were published in 1894, and in 1901 he published *Buddenbrooks* on the declining German bourgeoisie. During World War I he supported imperial Germany, which represented to him a conservative, romantic, harmonious soul in contrast to the shallow democracies fighting against her. After the war he was a main supporter of the Weimar Republic, which, as is well known, very much lacked such support. In 1924 *The Magic Mountain* was published, and in 1929 Thomas Mann was awarded the Nobel Prize for literature. In 1933, when Hitler came to power in Germany, he settled in Switzerland and became known for his anti-Nazi stand, which resulted in the annulment of his German citizenship and the burning of his books. In 1938 he emigrated to the United States where he completed the *Joseph* series and published *Dr. Faustus*. In 1952, during the McCarthy era, he left the United States and settled in Kilchberg, near Zürich, where he died in 1955.

The Magic Mountain was conceived in 1912 when Mann's wife Katia, following an attack of tuberculosis, was hospitalized in a forest sanatorium in Davos where he spent three weeks with her. The people he encountered in the sanatorium did not seem to recover, and he himself caught a troublesome bronchial cold, which inspired him to write a humorous novella on this experience that developed into the long novel. Katia Mann's memoirs reveal that many of the figures appearing in the novel were real: the ordinary Frau Stöhr, the door slamming Madame Chauchat, and the aggrieved mother lamenting the fatal illness of both her sons.[5] The central characters were not real persons, although similarities between the Italian Settembrini and Thomas Mann's brother, the writer Heinrich Mann, or between the Jewish Jesuit Naphta and the Marxist critic Georg Lukács have been noted.[6]

An analysis of the political theory in *The Magic Mountain* requires a word of caution; it is one of the most important and complex novels ever written and can be analyzed from many angles: as a spiritual autobiography, an historical novel, a fable about a declining European civilization, or a pedagogical novel within the tradition of the German "*Bildungsroman.*" A political analysis of this work obviously captures only a limited dimension of it.

The Magic Mountain is the tale of Hans Castorp, "a simple-minded though pleasing young man,"[7] who had just passed his exams in naval engineering and, when the book begins, is on his way to visit his cousin Joachim in the Berghof sanitarium in Davos. Hans does not resemble any of the characters we are familiar with from nineteenth-century literature; he is not a nobleman, a declining aristocrat, a proletarian, a landowner, or an individual confronting a corrupt political system. He is neither a hero nor a villain. Hans Castorp is a young, ordinary man, possessed with Nietzschean inquisitiveness, who lived an ordinary life with all its "duties, interests, cares and prospects"[8] in the world preceding the Great War.

The story of Hans Castorp, beginning with his climbing up the magic mountain, enables us to climb with him "upward into regions where he had never before drawn breath, and where he knew that unusual living conditions prevailed."[9] The living conditions in Berghof, where the entire book is placed, are unusual indeed. In that strange place, where snow falls in August, the world is observed, not experienced.[10] It is a cosmopolitan world inhabited by diverse types who share a common denominator: they are all sick. And their sickness lacks the delicacy with which maladies were often treated in novels: everybody is simply sick.[11]

The focus on sickness is crucial to an understanding of the fundamental view of body and soul in this novel; health and sickness, life and death, are strongly linked. One of the first pieces of information Hans Castorp is exposed to on the magic mountain concerns the bringing down of the bodies of the dead on bobsleds. When he visits Herr Hofrat Behrens, we are told that Hans had become an engineer by chance and could have actually become a physician, because "if you are interested in the body, you must be interested in disease."[12] Elsewhere he learns that "if one is interested in life, one must be particularly interested in death."[13] The human body, so admired in ancient Greece, in the Renaissance, or in modern sport culture, entirely loses its status in this book, as a result of scientific research which reveals its true essence: "The human body," Herr Behrens explains to the attentive Hans, "consists, much the larger part of it, of water. No more and no less than water, and

reduction of Man to Primary Substances

nothing to get wrought up about. The solid parts are only twenty-five per cent of the whole, and of that twenty are ordinary white of egg, protein, if you want to use a handsomer word. Besides that, a little fat and a little salt, that's about all."[14]

Man, the creature adored by all religions and philosophies, becomes in Hofrat's explanation no more than primary substances such as carbon, hydrogen, nitrogen, oxygen, sulphur, and phosphorous. In old age, the Hofrat explains, the flesh becomes tough because the collagen increases in the connective tissue – the lime, which is the most important constituent of the bones and cartilage, and in the muscle plasma we have an albumen called fibrin, which, when it coagulates in the muscular tissue, causes death. Thus, in this novel even death loses its romantic dignity and becomes a subject for "the anatomy of the grave,"[15] which reveals that it is nothing other than a process in which "you flow away, so to speak – remember all that water."[16]

Many theologians and philosophers would agree with Mann about the inferiority of the human body but would cherish the human consciousness. Hegel in particular influenced the placing of consciousness at the center stage of philosophy. In his *Phenomenology of Spirit*, this influential nineteenth-century German thinker described the dialectical process in which our consciousness of ourselves and of the world develops, with reason being the central factor shaping our lives. To Hegel, reason is a high form of self-consciousness that allows us to establish ethical social institutions and political orders.[17] But Hans Castorp, ordering scientific volumes to read in the long winter days at Berghof, learns that responses to stimuli, which represent a degree of consciousness, can already be found in the lowest animal forms, including those lacking a nervous system or a cerebrum. In a parody on Hegel, consciousness is defined as nothing but the senseless and aimless activity of matter turned self-conscious:

> Consciousness, then, was simply a function of matter organized into life; a function that in higher manifestations turned upon its avatar and became an effort to explore and explain the phenomenon it displayed – a hopeful-hopeless project of life to achieve self-knowledge, nature in recoil – and vainly, in the event, since she cannot be resolved in knowledge, nor life, when all is said, listen to itself.[18]

This quotation may be seen as directed at all those who arrogantly stressed the supremacy of reason over nature. Such arrogance could be found both in the church that subordinated the body to the soul and in humanism of the kind expressed by Voltaire when he protested, in the name of reason, against the Lisbon earthquake of 1755. In *The Magic Mountain*, many of the scientific and technological developments of the turn of the century, taken to symbolize the victory of human reason over nature, and promising to liberate civilization from the traditional constraints of nature and history, are presented as absurd, once seen from the perspective of the inquisitive Hans Castorp. In particular, the young man exposes the pretence of positivist sociology, redeeming psychoanalysis, and X-ray, one of the greatest achievements of medical science at the time.

The origins of sociology go back a long way, but the subjection of society to positivist study can be traced to the nineteenth century French scholar Auguste Comte who formulated the "law of human progress."[19] According to that law, each of our leading conceptions passes successively through three stages: a theological stage in which all phenomena are attributed to the immediate action of supernatural beings; a metaphysical stage in which abstract forces replace those metaphysical beings as causes of all phenomena; and third, a positivist stage in which "the mind has given over the vain search after absolute notions, the origin and destination of the universe, and the causes of phenomena, and applies itself to the study of their laws – that is, their invariable relations of succession and resemblance."[20] Comte proposed the combination of reasoning and observation as the means of knowledge both of physiological and social facts. He tied this positivism to the French Revolution, arguing that the shock of revolution was necessary for the foundation of a social science, since the basis of that science is the conception of human progress. Not only did the revolution bring that conception forward into sufficient prominence, the discourse it sparked led the public to look to positivism as a system containing in germ the ultimate solution to social problems.

Early sociologists have mostly accepted this link between positivism and social progress. As Alan Swingewood shows, positivism, embracing a belief in science as the foundation of all knowledge, the employment of statistical analysis in social theory, and the search for causal explanations of social phenomena, originated in the enlightenment and carried its fundamental tenets of philosophical individualism and human reason largely directed against the irrational powers of the absolutist state, organized religion, and residual social institutions.[21] In the early twentieth century, when the irrational powers of the masses were seen as more frightening than those of the state and religious institutions, the answer still resided with positivist sociology. Max Weber, Émile Durkheim, Karl Mannheim, and others developed a science of sociology that could be seen as an attempt to rescue mass society from the ills of charisma, conflict, and ideology.

The need to consider the wishes, passions, interests, and desires of the general public led to a body of literature revealing irrational trends in human affairs. Mass conduct was characterized by "unpredictability, violence, volatility and destructiveness."[22] Yet, while some thinkers ventured to consider the newly revealed irrationality as socially destructive, others, notably Durkheim, placed them into formulas consistent with the still prevalent notion of social progress. Mass sentiments became the staff holding social contracts together, and communal rituals – a unifying and energizing social force. As one of Durkheim's biographers notes, throughout his work on pre-modern, pre-literate social behaviors, the master sociologist remained "a man of science, committed to the view that reason should and could objectively ascertain, criticize, improve social conditions."[23]

However, while master sociologists pursued their endeavor with curiosity over mass behavior and concern for the fate of European civilization, many of their disciples turned the project into an experiment in analytical and quantitative science. The complex behavior of twentieth-century mass societies was to be captured by statistical methods whose usefulness seemed to be diminishing with their apparent methodological sophistication. The study of society, known as "social sciences," developed into what cultural historian Jacques Barzun calls "endless specialties."[24]

This trend would have remained of little concern had its practitioners not defined themselves as the vanguard of human progress. Social engineering, based on the achievements of social scientists, was seen as a sober alternative to the grand ideologies haunting humanity in the twentieth century. An alternative was desperately needed, especially in the era between the two world wars. But the statistically oriented economists, sociologists, and political scientists were incapable of providing it, because, as Barzun notes, their methods required too many abstractions: "It is not unfair to say that the present culture conducts its business largely like the inhabitants of Swift's island of Laputa, who hovered in the air over the solid earth beneath."[25]

The unease over the gap between the promise of sociology to become an advance guard protecting human progress and its dispersion into innumerable activities of questionable social validity is expressed by Hans Castorp in his encounter with the Italian Settembrini who represents a shallow version of Voltairean humanism. Settembrini considers buying Hofrat Behren for Christmas a newly projected encyclopedic work called *Sociology of Suffering*. This book, about which Hans Castorp learns from Settembrini in a reading room with oak paneling and a light, vaulted ceiling, contains the ambitious effort of the new science of sociology to apply a twentieth-century version of the enlightenment, in the form of positivistic research which improves the human condition by classifying and measuring it.

Curious Hans learns from Settembrini about the International League for the Organization of Progress that has composed the encyclopedia. The league deduced from Darwinian theory that man's profoundest natural impulse is in the direction of self-realization, and assembled those, like Settembrini, who sought satisfaction of this impulse and were willing to become co-workers in the cause of human progress:

> A comprehensive and scientifically executed programme has been drawn up, embracing all the projects for human improvement conceivable at the moment. We are studying the problem of our health as a race, and the means for combating the degeneration which is a regrettable accompanying phenomenon of our increasing industrialization.[26]

The aims are broad: to provide people with access to universities, resolve the class conflicts and do away with national conflicts, but the means are those familiar to every social scientist: discussion groups, sending material to progressive political parties, and establishment of international periodicals – "monthly reviews, which contain articles in three or four languages on the subject of the progressive evolution of civilized humanity."[27]

The critique of the ambitions of sociology reaches a peak when Settembrini discusses a League meeting in Barcelona at which the encyclopedia was conceived:

[T]he League for the Organization of Progress, mindful of its task of furthering human happiness – in other words, of combating human suffering by the available social methods, to the end of finally eliminating it altogether; mindful also of the fact that this lofty task can only be accomplished by the aid of sociology, the end and aim of which is the perfect State, the League, in session at Barcelona, determined upon the publication of a series of volumes bearing the general title: *The Sociology of Suffering*. It should be the aim of the series to classify human suffering according to classes and categories, and to treat it systematically and exhaustively. You ask what is the use of classification, arrangement, systematization? I answer you: order and simplification are the first steps toward the mastery of a subject – the actual enemy is the unknown.[28]

The novelist exposes the gap between sociology's ambitions and the simplification with which it treats its subject matter – the human condition. Scholars, research assistants, statisticians and others who joined in the twentieth-century positivist endeavor accompanying the modern industrial state have often considered themselves, after Karl Mannheim's *Ideology and Utopia*, as "co-workers" in an updated enlightenment project. Mannheim, deeply concerned over the destructive nature of communism and fascism, proposed in 1929 a "sociology of knowledge" whose practitioners overcome the fundamental falsities and authoritarianism of the age's ideological structures by an open-minded investigation of these structures as part of an overall sociological project.[29] But Hans Castorp conveys his unease over the simplifying nature of sociology's research methods, often expressed by first-year students before they are socialized into the field, as well as the scant power of sociology to enlighten the human race. No wonder that Settembrini, suggesting to the Berghof's residents that they buy this encyclopedia as a gift, "found only one person to agree with him, a book-dealer who sat at Hermine Kleefeld's table."[30]

That unease increases when Castorp is exposed to psychoanalysis, an even greater promise for the liberation of civilization. In *The Passion of the Western Mind*, Richard Tarnas highlights that promise. Psychoanalysis, he writes, served as the virtual epiphany for the early-twentieth-century mind as it brought to light the archaeological depths of the psyche, thereby representing a brilliant culmination of the Enlightenment project, bringing even human consciousness under the light of rational investigation.[31] Tarnas realizes that this was only part of the impact of psychoanalysis, for it also undermined the entire Enlightenment project. This was done by the revelation of Freud, who developed psychoanalysis and turned it into a world movement, that below or beyond the rational mind existed an overwhelmingly potent repository of non-rational forces. With Freud, "the Darwinian struggle with nature took on new dimensions, as man was now constrained to live in eternal struggle with his own nature."[32]

In other words, Freud's penetration into the depths of the human psyche – the dreams, the neurosis, the sexual drives, the myths, etc. – while condemning individuals to a self-conscious existence, had also liberated them. As Carl Schorske puts it in his study of *fin-de-siècle* Vienna, "Freud gave his fellow-liberals an a-historical theory of man and society that could make bearable a political world spun out of orbit and beyond control."[33]

Thomas Mann was well aware of the liberating power of psychoanalysis. In a speech he delivered in Vienna in 1936 on Freud's eightieth birthday, he said:

> We shall one day recognize in Freud's life-work the cornerstone for the building of a new anthropology and therewith of a new structure, to which many stones are being brought up today, which shall be the future dwelling of a wiser and freer humanity.[34]

The humanism based on Freud, Mann believed, will differ from the humanism of the past in its different relation to the powers of the lower world, the unconscious, the id: "a relation bolder, freer, blither, productive of a riper art than any possible in our neurotic, fear-ridden, hate-ridden world."[35] Yet, the novelist objected to the turning of psychoanalysis into a myth, emphasizing instead the skepticism and modesty it implied to him:

> The analytic revelation is a revolutionary force. With it a blithe skepticism has come into the world, a mistrust that unmasks all the schemes and subterfuges of our own souls.[36]

As is well known, the dissemination of psychoanalysis in twentieth-century culture did not involve such skepticism and modesty. Despite vast critique of Freud's assumptions and statements, the preoccupation with the unconscious, which already excited the public mind in *fin-de-siècle* Europe, was accompanied by an aura of mysticism as it developed into a main trait in twentieth-century literature, art, and popular culture. Freud has become bigger than life. To quote English poet W. H. Auden: "to us he is no more a person/now but a whole climate of opinion/under which we conduct our different lives."[37]

In a special issue of the *Annual of Psychoanalysis* in 2001 devoted to Freud's impact on literature and literary criticism, drama, cinema, visual arts, religious studies, the human sciences, etc., the editors claim that we see ourselves and everything around us from a perspective that did not exist in the pre-Freudian era.

> We know that all people have motivations of which they are unaware. A person's inner life (dreams, fantasies, private thoughts) is as important as the external life.... Today there may be as many people as ever who find sexuality disquieting, but there is no longer a pretence that it is an incidental part of life. In law attention is paid to a defendant's state of mind. In the cinema even action films are expected to give some consideration to psychological motivation.[38]

And one Internet site has it that "[m]ore than Einstein or Watson and Crick, more than Hitler or Lenin, Roosevelt or Kennedy, more than Picasso, Eliot, or Stravinsky, more than the Beatles or Bob Dylan, Freud's influence on modern culture has been profound and long-lasting."[39]

The Magic Mountain exposes the myth accompanying psychoanalysis. Hans Castorp warns us not to be entrapped by its magic spell, as so many mythical cults in the past have failed to redeem us. In a chapter entitled "analysis," Hans listens to a lecture by Dr. Krokowski, whose special field is the psychoanalysis of love. The audience is unusually attentive: "Many of the guests had their hands curved behind their ears; some even held the hand in the air half-way thither, as though arrested midway in the gesture by the strength of their concentration."[40] This attentiveness is related to the innovation introduced by psychoanalysis, allowing the public mention of sexual themes dressed in pseudo-scientific terms:

> It was a bit odd, to be sure, listening to a lecture on such a theme, when previously Hans Castorp's courses had dealt only with such matters as geared transmission in ship-building. No, really, how did one go about to discuss a subject of this delicate and private nature, in broad daylight, before a mixed audience? Dr. Krokowski did it by adopting a mingled terminology, partly poetic and partly erudite; ruthlessly scientific, yet with a vibrating, singsong delivery, which impressed young Hans Castorp as being unsuitable, but may have been the reason why the ladies looked flushed and the gentlemen flicked their ears to make them hear better.[41]

The religious overtones of the experience are apparent in the portrayal of Krokowski as a biblical figure dressed in a frock coat, negligee collar, sandals, and gray woolen socks, delivering a biblical sermon, inflicting the fear of God on the audience: "He demolished illusions, he was ruthlessly enlightened, he relentlessly destroyed all faith in the dignity of silver hairs and the innocence of the sucking babe."[42] The struggle between love as an unreliable instinct prone to error and perversion, and chastity as a corrective force promoting order and conformity, is discussed, as is the tendency of love, once suppressed, to reappear in the form of illness.

As this goes on, Hans Castorp's attention is easily diverted to Madame Chauchet, who is seated in front of him. Boredom is the main message he conveys to us as the sermon goes on and on, with Krokowski, his arms outstretched and his head on one side, reminiscent of Christ on the cross:

> It seemed that at the end of his lecture Dr. Krokowski was making propaganda for psycho-analysis; with open arms he summoned all and sundry to come unto him. "Come unto me," he was saying, though not in those words, "come unto me, all ye who are weary and heavy-laden." And he left no doubt of his conviction that all those present *were* weary and heavy-laden. He spoke of secret suffering, of shame and sorrow, of the redeeming power of the analytic. He advocated the bringing of light into the unconscious

mind and explained how the abnormality was metamorphosed into the conscious emotion; he urged them to have confidence; he promised relief.[43]

The same kind of irony versus the great promises of the age can be found when Hans Castorp is introduced to medical technologies intended to cure the sick. "X-ray anatomy, you know, triumph of the age."[44] says the Hofrat Behren when the two cousins, Hans and Joachim, visit him in Berghof's X-ray laboratory. Hans is both enchanted and fearful upon his first visit to an X-ray darkroom:

> It smelled very odd in here, the air was filled with a sort of stale ozone. The built-in structure, projecting between the two black-hung windows, divided the room into two unequal parts. Hans Castorp could distinguish physical apparatus. Lenses, switchboards, towering measuring-instruments, a box like a camera on a rolling stand, glass diapositives in rows set in the walls. Hard to say whether this was a photographic studio, a dark-room, or an inventor's workshop and technological witches' kitchen.[45]

The notion of science and technology as originating in a "witches' kitchen" is a common theme in early twentieth-century literature. More than reflecting an anti-technological attitude, it indicated a degree of fascination with science and technology. The capacity of the market and the state to embrace technological development to the extent they did was due to public fascination with the images associated with it: the racing car, the nuclear mushroom, the space rocket, "star wars," the glittering computer screen-protector, etc. The lengthy descriptions of medical science and technology in *The Magic Mountain* may have also contributed to that fascination, but Hans Castorp sends us an effective warning. Just like the biblical warning "Thou shalt not look at me and live," we are forced to look at ourselves while we are playing God.

In a chapter entitled "Sudden Enlightenment," Hans Castorp is literally taking a look at himself. The more the laboratory is presented to him in detail, including the entire equipment, motions, smells, even the doctors' jokes ("I expect, Castorp, you feel a little nervous about exposing your inner

We Are Not Immortal / 27

self to our gaze? Don't be alarmed, we preserve all the amenities"),[46] the more unfamiliar the setting becomes. We the readers following Castorp are forced to confront ourselves as we undergo, as part of the triumph of the age, the transformation from "Man" to "God." And we are left terrified. What is so terrifying is not the technology itself, which seems mild and tame compared to later technologies, such as the atomic bomb, but the realization that its development and use implies the passing of a threshold beyond which innocent life is no longer possible. With the X-ray machine and similar inventions, the human race has eaten from the fruit of the tree of knowledge and can no longer hide behind a veil of ignorance about its fate. The "sudden enlightenment" in the chapter's title, refers to Hans Castorp's realization that he is going to die.

This dispels the illusion that the forces of nature can be tamed for the benefit of humanity without serious consequences. The scene in which Joachim is being X-rayed resembles Dante's inferno:

> "Now, for the space of two seconds, fearful powers were in play – streams of thousands, of a hundred thousand of volts, Hans Castorp seemed to recall – which were necessary to pierce through solid matter. They could hardly be confined to their office, they tried to escape through other outlets: there were explosions like pistol-shots, blue sparks on the measuring apparatus; long lightnings crackled along the walls. Somewhere in the room appeared a red light, like a threatening eye, and a phial in Joachim's rear filled with green. Then everything grew quiet...."[47]

And when Hans himself presses his chest against the X-ray board, he understands how much he actually changes with the technology. "We must first accustom the eyes," the Hofrat is saying to him in the darkness, "We must get big pupils, like a cat's, to see what we want to see. You understand, our everyday eyesight would not be good enough for our purposes. We have to banish the bright daylight and its pretty pictures out of our minds."[48]

The cost involved in taming the forces of nature remains undefined. It resides mainly in the power given to humanity to see through the illusions that protected it in the past. Once Hans Castorp is given the opportunity to see his brother's honor-loving heart in an X-ray picture, an illusion is gone

Technology [handwritten annotation above "condition"]

and he finds himself in the condition of the long dead woman "who had been endowed or afflicted with a heavy gift, which she bore in all humility: namely, that the skeletons of persons about to die would appear before her."[49] It becomes very clear how much the power given to us by technology requires choices we may not be willing or prepared to make.

Indeed, while life-curing and life-extending technologies are becoming commonplace, the choices they force upon us are still mainly handled by avoidance. The medical doctor, for example, who, like the above woman, is given control over life and death by machines extending life artificially is mostly reluctant to make the necessary decisions, and so are the courts, the church, the press, etc. This condition was foreseen by Hans Castorp's concern over what he saw in the X-ray lab, or more precisely, over the very fact that he saw it. Standing in the dark, Hans Castorp began to doubt, as do so many individuals in the technological age, whether he should have stood there at all gazing at the secrets of nature, for he understood what he was looking at: "he looked into his own grave."[50]

Hans Castorp also exposes the difficulty the prevailing ideologies had in coping with the politics of the twentieth century. A large part of the book consists of a conversation he listens to between Settembrini and Naphta who represent opposed clusters of ideas expressed in the history of political philosophy.

Who are the two disputants? Settembrini, the mellifluous democrat, has been compared to a character out of a Heinrich Mann novel, and Naphta, the repellent provocateur, to a character worthy of Dostoevsky or Joseph Conrad.[51] The Italian Settembrini, whose grandfather was a political agitator in Milan dedicated to national liberation, whose father was a classical scholar and humanist, and who himself is a resident of the Berghof sanitarium, advocates a liberal nationalism of the Mazzini school based on belief in progress and reason. He thinks that the development of science, based on pure knowledge, provides for the victory of Man over nature as well as for the coming together of peoples in a world in which prejudice would be replaced by fraternity and happiness. Settembrini advocates the right of nations to self-determination and is convinced that once all nations are granted freedom and independence, they will be capable of living in a peaceful world. He never doubts the existence of the human spirit, deriving its existence from Rousseau and other eighteenth-century thinkers who believe the individual to be originally good, happy, and without sin. Social errors have corrupted and perverted humanity, but with the advancement of knowledge, a good, happy, and sinless existence is assured.

Naphta, the small, thin, ugly Jesuit of Jewish origin, with his hooked nose dominating his face, his narrow, pursed mouth and pale-gray eyes, expresses the quest for redemption underlying political theory since Rousseau, especially Marxism.

To him, Rousseau's ideal is nothing but a sophisticated adaptation of the Church's doctrine of the fall from the City of God that ought to be restored. Naphta does not believe in pure knowledge; pure science is to him a myth. The vehicle of knowledge is faith, and intellect plays a secondary role – that of exploring the human will, which is always in existence, even in the formulation of science's own rules of evidence. Truth coincides with the human interest, with the quest of redemption. Any theoretical science that has no practical application to that salvation is therefore insignificant and cannot serve as a basis of hope. In contrast to Settembrini, who seeks the liberation of humankind from the unenlightened ideas of the historical church, he thinks that it was not the church that defended darkness but rather a natural science that tried to advance without taking human salvation into account.

The application of these contrasting ideas to politics exposes the impasse that twentieth-century political theory had reached. Settembrini argues against Naphta that the introduction of the idea of redemption in a political context gives rise to the greatest evils because the salvation of the state becomes the main standard:

> The good, the true, and the just, is that which advantages the State: its safety, its honour, its power form the sole criterion of morality. Well and good. But mark that herewith you fling open the door for every sort of crime to enter; while as for human truth, individual justice, democracy, you can see what will become of them —[52]

But Naphta argues the opposite: it was the belief in God that kept the state in its place while the Renaissance, by abolishing the dualism between man and God and by developing the notion of the cosmos as infinite, allowed for the sanctification of the state. Settembrini's answer consists mainly of Voltairean slogans:

> To find in the Renaissance the origin of State-worship – what bastard logic! The achievements wrung from the past – I use the word literally, my dear sir – wrung from the past by the Renaissance and the intellectual revival are personality, freedom, and the rights of man.[53]

Hans and Joachim, the bystanders, meet these slogans of the enlightenment with approval but Naphta raises a hard point. While admitting that the liberal norms of individualism and the humanistic conception of citizenship were products of the Renaissance, he reminds Settembrini that the Renaissance is a thing of the past, "while the feet of those who will deal them the *coup de grâce* are already before the door." [54] These words, published in 1924, are perhaps the strongest in *The Magic Mountain*. The Jesuit announces that the principle of freedom has outlived its usefulness and adherence to it, by the educational system for example, may provide it with a temporary rhetorical advantage, but is hopeless:

> All educational organizations worthy of the name have always recognized what must be the ultimate and significant principle of pedagogy: namely the absolute mandate, the iron bond, discipline, sacrifice, the renunciation of the ego, the curbing of the personality. And lastly, it is an unloving miscomprehension of youth to believe that it finds its pleasure in freedom: its deepest pleasure lies in obedience.... Liberation and development of the individual are not the key to our age, they are not what our age demands. What it needs, what it wrestles after, what it will create – is Terror.[55]

As the conversation progresses, both discussants bring up their models of the just state. Settembrini expresses in diminishing vigor his vision of the enlightenment while Naphta, in a blend of Roman Catholicism and revolutionary Marxism, proposes equality and fraternity to be achieved by a proletariat replacing the capitalistic system with a violent version of the universal Christian state. Naphta claims that papal religious zeal burns within the proletariat and that it will therefore not refrain from the shedding of blood. Its task is to strike terror in order to redeem the world and make it sacred, stateless, and classless.

Where is Hans Castorp, the simple fellow, the potential beneficiary of the ideological schemes, in all that? After listening to the endless exchange of statements and counter-statements, he comes to the conclusion that none of the models makes sense, that it is impossible to judge which of the contenders is right and which is wrong, which is a sinner and which is a believer. And it becomes clear what the consequences of such failure to reach agreement on the truth are:

> They broke off at last. There were no limits to the subject – but they could not go on for ever. The three guests of the Berghof took their way home, and the two disputants had to go into the cottage together, the one to seek his silken cell, the other his humanistic cubby-hole with the pulpit-desk and the water-bottle. Hans Castorp betook himself to his balcony, his ears full of the hurly-burly and the clashing of arms, as the army of Jerusalem and that of Babylon, under the *dos banderas*, came on in battle array, and met each other midst tumult and shoutings.[56]

By considering ideological discourse to be deadlocked and war as the only consequence of that deadlock, Thomas Mann seemed to join a trend among European intellectuals described by cultural historian Ronald Stromberg as a quest for "redemption by war."[57] This trend consisted of greeting the outbreak of World War I with enthusiasm, hoping that it would bring resurrection, purification, and liberation to an intellectual community that sensed a loss of feeling, community, and clear direction. Although this trend was universal, it was particularly common among German intellectuals who, as Martha Hanna shows, believed that the war "would usher in a new age for the nation, an age that, free of politics and internal division, would be capable of producing genuine social cohesion."[58] Liberals, socialists, humanists, and cosmopolitans shared with nationalists the feeling that Europe was entangled not only in political but also in intellectual deadlock, and the war was expected to break the impasse, construct a new world in which one side would win and another lose, and enable Europe to follow a clear path again.

Thomas Mann was accused of being one of those intellectuals because of his expectation during the war that the German soul would emerge strong, proud, free, and happy, and because of his idealization of Joachim, Hans Castorp's soldier brother, who is indeed the only positive figure in *The Magic Mountain*. This idealization can be found in the novel; Mann's description of soldiers in war is, in fact, quite romantic ("Ah, this young blood, with its knapsacks and bayonets, its mud-befouled boots and clothing!").[59] But the accusation seems less justified when we consider Hans Castorp's private sphere.

There has always been a great difference between the discourse on war in the public and private spheres. It is one thing to support war and another to send one's own child to fight in it. In this novel, the readers are led in the cruelest manner through both levels of discourse. War may be the majestic solution to the political deadlock in Europe, but we also follow Hans Castorp, so familiar to us by now, when sent, in the last pages of the novel, to fight in the wars of Europe. Here, the meeting between public and private becomes unbearable, as it does for every individual and family having ever had to experience war, however just that war may have seemed in the public discourse. Hans Castorp, disappointed by all political ideas of the modern era, goes out to fight in a redeeming war, but, as in war, he vanishes out of sight in the tumult, rain, and dusk, and we are given no guarantee of his safe return.

A Bureaucratic Nightmare

Modernity is associated with bureaucracy. Bureaucracy – the routinization of public action in hierarchical structures – has always existed in human societies, but while in ancient Egypt, China or Czarist Russia it was associated with traditional and charismatic forms of leadership, in modern times it has become dominant in itself. Max Weber, the theorist of bureaucracy, considered such dominance inevitable. He believed it was necessitated – paradoxically – by the development of mass democracy. The need to assure equality before the law in mass democracies, in contrast to the democratic self-government of small societies, he wrote, calls for "the abstract regularity of the execution of authority."[1]

Weber, inspired by Bismarck's Prussia, spelled out the components of a model of bureaucracy and presented it as the climax of the "routinization of charisma." He showed how authority was defined by rules and regulations confining public activity to fixed jurisdictional areas. The regular activities required for the purposes of the bureaucratically governed structure, he explained, are distributed in a fixed way as official duties, the authority to give commands required for the discharge of these duties is distributed in a stable way, and methodical provision is made for the regular and continuous fulfillment of these duties by recruitment of qualified personnel.

Only persons who have the generally regulated qualifications to serve are employed, and they are placed in a hierarchical structure. The structuring of authority in a hierarchy, which can be found in any bureaucracy, is supposed to lead to an orderly system in which lower offices are supervised by higher offices and the governed people appeal decisions of lower offices to higher ones "in a definitely regulated manner."[2] The strict regulation of a bureaucracy assures its smooth operation beyond the contingencies, or life span, of the individuals comprising it. Regulation is enhanced by the submission of instructions and other organizational communications in writing and by the preservation of the organization's files in their original form.

The abstract nature of this model is striking. As Weber, born into a political family, knew quite well, bureaucratic life always involves conflicts of interest, power struggles, arbitrary decisions, and informal communications, which makes it hard to conceive of authority as routine and regulated. Yet this model became a cornerstone in twentieth-century organizational theory apparently because it provided a structure that promised to solve the problems caused by the mixture of the private and public spheres. Weber was explicit:

> In principle, the modern organization of the civil service separates the bureau from the private domicile of the official, and, in general, bureaucracy segregates official activity as something distinct from the sphere of private life.[3]

Weber expected the separation of the private and public to assure that goal-oriented public action replace private greed, and public property be used for the advancement of society rather than for the benefit of individual officials. He was aware that public property had often been robbed by corrupt political officials and leading entrepreneurs, but believed that ultimately a bureaucratic authority structure would prevail in which "the executive office is separated from the household, business from private correspondence, and business assets from private fortunes."[4] In that structure, economic and political enterprises are managed by well-trained experts and specialized office managers. These experts devote their full time and attention to the organizational tasks, and are familiar with rules of management that are "more or less stable, more or less exhaustive, and which can be learnt."⁵ To him, this form of structuring authority seemed permanent:

> Once it is fully established, bureaucracy is among those social structures which are the hardest to destroy. Bureaucracy is *the* means of carrying "community action" over into rationally ordered "societal action". Therefore, as an instrument for "societalizing" relations of power, bureaucracy has been and is a power instrument of the first order – for the one who controls the bureaucratic apparatus.⁶

Nobody has doubted the power of bureaucracy, or the contention that it is practically unshatterable. The question was whether it could be controlled, and whether a hierarchical structure marked by specialization and expertise is consistent with democracy. Weber himself was ambivalent about the ability to reconcile bureaucracy and democracy. On the one hand, he welcomed the leveling of social differences when officials are recruited on the basis of merit and expertise; it liberates modern administration from existing social, material or honorific preferences and ranks. On the other hand, he was aware of the dehumanizing effect of bureaucratic structures:

> The individual bureaucrat cannot squirm out of the apparatus in which he is harnessed. In contrast to the honorific or avocational "notable", the professional bureaucrat is chained to his activity by his entire material and ideal existence. In the great majority of cases, he is only a single cog in an ever-moving mechanism which prescribes to him an essentially fixed route of march.⁷

Although Weber and his disciples, theoretical and empirical sociologists as well as experts on management and organizational behavior, could avoid spelling out the normative implications of this effect, those destined to serve as cogs in the growing bureaucratic structures of the twentieth century could not. The question of bureaucracy was one of the hardest to cope with. On the one hand, the routinization of charisma and the construction of legal-rational systems providing a degree of stability and predictability seemed warranted in view of the rise of charismatic leaders like Lenin and Hitler. On the other hand, the evils of these leaders could be attributed not only to charisma but also to the bureaucratic structures surrounding them. The world wars, although inspired by charismatic leaders, were fought by huge military-industrial systems run by faceless experts. Moreover, while leaders are dispensable, these systems seemed permanent and raised deep worry over the increasing subordination of private behavior to organizational routine.

This is where Joseph K. comes in. *The Trial*'s main character demonstrates the horrors the individual is subjected to in the bureaucratic state: uncertainty, loneliness, helplessness, and fear. Although not confined only to bureaucratic structures, the Kafkaean condition is best described in relation to them.

Franz Kafka was born in Bohemia in 1883. He studied law and was employed in those cold, gray offices constructed at the turn of the century to house its bureaucracies. His main position was with the Workers' Accident Insurance Institute for the Kingdom of Bohemia in Prague where he prepared such reports as "the bulletin for 1907–8 on compulsory insurance in the building trade and on motor insurance."[8] In order to fulfill his unexciting job, he took courses in workers' insurance, the structure of ministerial departments, and statistics. One of his biographers, Ronald Hayman, described the office building in which he worked as "so massive and dignified, that the poor invalids and workmen summoned to collect pensions or receive compensation for injury usually looked bewildered and intimidated from the first moment of glimpsing the porter with his enormous beard."[9] No wonder the "routinization of charisma" seemed uninspiring to the insurance clerk.

Kafka was a member of the "Prague Circle," a group of writers, most of them Jewish, who lived in Prague, "a very metropolis indeed thanks to its being bilingual, to its variety of creeds and classes, and thanks to its often having played a decisive part over the centuries in the determination of the fate of Europe."[10] Jewish intellectuals in Prague enjoyed its cosmopolitan nature. They were educated in general German-language schools, lived a bourgeois life, and were mostly removed from traditional Jewish learning and customs. Within this cosmopolitan setting, they encountered three competing national movements active in Prague – Czech nationalism,

German nationalism and Jewish nationalism (Zionism). The encounter with nationalism within a cosmopolitan setting influenced them in a unique way. Prague Circle novels, such as Max Brod's *Reubeni Fürst der Juden*, Franz Werfel's *The Forty Days of Musa Dagh*, or Franz Kafka's *The Trial*, portrayed a more sober model of the nation-state than those found in contemporary works describing modern European nationalism with romantic overtones.

The Prague circle viewed the nation-state not as a "promised land" but as a leviathan whose messianic rhetoric was secondary to *realpolitik*. In national movements seeking independence, the state is usually defined as redeeming to individuals and whole societies, but as Brod's fifteenth-century false prophet Reubeni learns in an imaginary meeting with Machiavelli, as Werfel's German pastor Lepsius, attempting to help the Armenians in World War I, learns in a meeting with Turkey's Minister of War, Enver Pasha, and as Kafka's Joseph K. learns from his own endeavors, the messiah does not reside in the bureaucratic apparatus of the state. That apparatus stands by itself, devoid of any redeeming power.

This attitude, stripping the bureaucratic apparatus of the state from the romantic overtones attributed to the state by modern nationalism, made a difference in 1914. As stated before, Europe's intellectuals greeted the breakout of World War I with enthusiasm, believing that victory by their respective countries would liberate Europe from the political and intellectual deadlocks it found itself in. The Great War was expected to solve the political and intellectual problems of Europe. It led instead to Europe's decline and to the rise of totalitarianism. Like a contagious disease, it spread to all continents and seas. It was expected to be a short, swift war but lasted four years and wiped out a whole generation. Nations fought each other to the bitter end, and that end was bitter for all of them. This is why so many emerging from it beaten and broken could find inspiration in Kafka who did not share in the enthusiasm of 1914.

The sick, suicidal, self-hating Prague writer watched the nationalistic outbursts – the parades, the speeches, the military bands, the girls sticking flowers into the soldiers' bayonets – with apathy. As indicated in his diary, when the war broke out he had a different perspective than the cheering crowds of Europe:

> August 2. Germany has declared war on Russia – swimming in the afternoon ... August 6. The artillery that marched across the Graben. Flowers, shouts of hurrah! I am more broken down than recovered. An empty vessel, still intact yet already in the dust among the broken fragments; or already in fragments yet still raged among those that are intact. Full of lies, hate and envy ... I discover in myself nothing but pettiness, indecision, envy and hatred against those who are fighting and whom I passionately wish everything evil.[11]

If Thomas Mann's *The Magic Mountain* is the tale of the pre-1914 world that fell into disaster, Kafka's *The Trial*, composed in the first weeks of World War I, may be seen as the direct expression of that disaster. Thomas Mann considered two ideological options – Settembrini's belief in humanity and Naphta's search for redemption – showing both as incapable to provide a solution to the world of the twentieth century. To Kafka, however, there existed no options at all. In reading his works we are placed in the realm of the nightmares of a civilization blowing itself up.

It is hard to place the novel within known literary genres. It has been considered a book without genre, a mystification of meaninglessness, a religious crime novel, a fantasy about the guilt of "organizational man," or rather of an individual refusing to yield to the organization. Joseph K. has been analyzed as a person lacking any sensitivity to the world surrounding him or, to the contrary, as a moral, inquisitive individual. The novel had been compared to the great works of Kabbalah, even to the writings of the ancient prophets. "Kafka knew," wrote George Steiner in reference to Kafka's prophecy of the totalitarian state and its concentration camps.

> Kafka's misery as one coerced into writing, his almost hysterical diffidence before mundane authorship, are the facsimile, perhaps consciously arrived at, of the attempts of the prophets to evade the intolerable burden of their seeing.[12]

But *The Trial* is also about political theory, for it deals with power, authority, and law. Jane Bennett writes that by magnifying a set of fleeting experiences, Kafka's stories disclose a less familiar modality of power, and by depicting power as a variable field that mocks stabilizing description, the stories throw into relief theoretical frameworks brought to the text by reader or character.[13]

For instance, power is expected to be exercised by actor A over actor B and political theorists preoccupy themselves with the normative questions involved: what are the limits on the uses of power, what are the commitments of A towards B, what legitimate options are available to B to become liberated from the control of A, etc. However, in *The Trial* there is power exercised on B (or rather on K.) but there exists no visible A. Throughout the novel, power is exercised but its source is never revealed.

"Someone must have been telling lies about Joseph K.," the novel begins, "for without having done anything wrong he was arrested one fine morning."[14] When the novel ends, we still have no clue who that "someone" may have been, who lied; was it a person, a group, or an organization, did it really occur, who was behind the arrest and why. Power is exerted throughout the book but the sources and components of power, or the nature of the relationship between the actors, if one exists, are never revealed.

When the source and nature of power are not revealed, there is no way of knowing if that source is legitimate. Kafka thus abolishes the relationship between crime and punishment. In a world in which power is exercised by anonymous authority structures, the punishment inflicted by these structures becomes arbitrary, if only because of their complexity. When we are summoned to court, we usually assume there is a reason for it related to our deeds. However, in *The Trial* this assumption loses ground. We have no idea whether Joseph K. is guilty or not and whether his guilt is relevant at all.

Thus, Joseph K. expresses the ambivalence individuals feel vis-à-vis the exercise of power on a daily basis. One gets into a government office and cannot predict what will be found there: Will the offices be occupied or empty? Will the clerks be busy? If they are busy, are they working on the tasks assigned to them by law? And if they are not busy, will they behave politely or rudely? When they are polite, is there some trickery or intrigue behind their courtesy, and when they are rude, is it one's own fault? When a complaint is filed against rude behavior and some clerk is punished while the entire system remains intact, does it matter? The difficulty of drawing any conclusions in the circumstances of modern bureaucracy is apparent on every page of this book, which can be read as a statement about the implications of the subjection of one individual – Joseph K. – to the routines of bureaucracy.

We hardly know anything about Joseph K.; even his full surname is not revealed. Our introduction to his private sphere does not include revelations about feelings, emotions, or desires. K. is an individual but our exposure to his individualism is limited due to his symbiosis with the bureaucratic structure he is part of. More than representing a real person, the anonymous Joseph K. is a parody of "political man" as the term was understood in nineteenth-century European civilization, that is, a person who has grown up in an orderly polity that assures a predictable set of norms. A key phrase can be found at the beginning when K., subjected to a surprise arrest, wonders what authority resides behind this arrest, as if authority in a modern context can be established at all:

> Who could these men be? What were they talking about? What authority could they represent? K. lived in a country with a legal constitution, there was universal peace, all the laws were in force; who dared seize him in his own dwelling?[15]

The expectation that the rule of law will prevail is not abandoned: "Who are you?" K. asks the man who appears one morning in his bedroom, as the totalitarian state would a few decades later. But as it turns out, this question is irrelevant; individuals have no chance to make sense of the authority surrounding them and the laws by which it operates. This is not because the bureaucratic structures in which authority is routinized are extraordinary but because they are not. The question "who are you?" is ignored, as though the appearance of a public official at one's bed one bright morning has become a routine.

Communication between Joseph K. and other individuals is confined to the constraints of hierarchy, with no meeting of souls:

> 'You can't go out, you are arrested.' 'So it seems', said K. 'But what for?' he added. 'We are not authorized to tell you that.'[16]

The confinement of human relations to organizational roles is total; everybody is part of the organization. Communication is conducted between individuals but it leads nowhere because individual concerns are not open to negotiations. Joseph K.'s communications are smooth and polite, but this only highlights their constrained nature. The bureaucracy is a stronger force than the clerks comprising it:

> Do you think you'll bring this fine case of yours to a speedier end by wrangling with us, your warders, over papers and warrants? We are humble subordinates who can scarcely find our way through a legal document and have nothing to do with your case except to stand guard over you for ten hours a day and draw our pay for it. That's all we are, but we're quite capable of grasping the fact that the high authorities we serve, before they would order such an arrest as this, must be quite well informed about the reasons for the arrest and the person of the prisoner.[17]

The authorities may be informed about the prisoner, but the prisoner has no way of knowing whether they really are and what it is they know or don't know. This subjects Joseph K. to the limited authority of lower clerks who make no difference in the long run but whose behavior becomes the main determinant of his fortune, as is often the case in prison where one's fate depends on the mood of particular guards:

> If you continue to have as good luck as you have had in the choice of your warders, then you can be confident of the final result.[18]

Upon his arrest, K. does not understand this truth and must be told that the warder–prisoner relationship is now dominant in his life:

> 'But how can I be under arrest? And particularly in such a ridiculous fashion? 'So now you're beginning it all over again?' said the warder, dipping a slice of bread and butter into the honey-pot. 'We don't answer such questions.' 'You'll have to answer them,' said K., 'Here are my papers, now show me yours, and first of all your warrant for arresting me.' 'Oh, good Lord,' said the warder. 'If you would only realize your position, and if you wouldn't insist

on uselessly annoying us two, who probably mean better by you and stand closer to you than any other people in the world.'[19]

This is undoubtedly true. There is nobody closer to K. than the officials he negotiates with. No social group exists that mediates between him and the bureaucratic apparatus. In the past, traditional and charismatic authority structures allowed individuals of high rank or class to overcome legal and other constraints through contacts with "their own." K. is tempted to establish such contacts but they no longer exist: "A few words with a man on my own level of intelligence would make everything far clearer than hours of talk with these two," but the system knows better. One's social contacts become unreliable once the law has put its hand on a person, however powerful and well-connected that person feels he is:

> 'Hasterer, the lawyer, is a personal friend of mine,' he said, 'may I telephone to him?' 'Certainly, replied the Inspector, 'but I don't see what sense there would be in that, unless you have some private business of your own to consult him about.'[20]

Not only does K. lack personal contacts and group connections to help him; he cannot count on popular support either. This is apparent when he has his "day in court" and is given the opportunity to say it all, to express what every person exposed to the overwhelming power of anonymous bureaucracy would want to say:

> '[T]here can be no doubt that behind all the actions of this court of justice, that is to say in my case, behind my arrest and today's interrogation, there is a great organization at work. An organization which not only employs corrupt warders, oafish Inspectors, and Examining Magistrates of whom the best that can be said is that they recognize their own limitations, but also has at its disposal a judicial hierarchy of high, indeed of the highest rank, with an indispensable and numerous retinue of servants, clerks, police, and other assistants, perhaps even hangmen, I do not shrink from that word.'[21]

But a small disruption at the corner of the room in which this statement is made diverts everybody's attention away from the speaker who remains, as we so often do, in his isolation. The small disruption is enough to divert attention from K.'s sermon because his personal views were never important to anybody in the first place, but the disruption is significant in an additional way; it signifies the main feature missing in the Weberian bureaucratic model. Joseph K. is never exposed to grand events, just to small disturbances. This is where the nightmare of this novel originates. Bureaucracy does not use dramatically coercive means – it mostly operates according to routines set by law. Only small disruptions occur – someone is not found where we expect him to be, someone is found where we don't expect her to be, or something just doesn't seem quite right.

For instance, K. finds on a judge's desk books containing pornographic material and there is no way to tell whether this is intentional, a matter of neglect, a hidden message, or just one of the complexities of a modern world. It is the tiny disruptions that matter. In this particular case, it was caused when a man pulled a washerwoman into a corner by the door and clasped her in his arms. Big organizations may get out of control for reasons, known as "human errors," that are no less trivial.

The bureaucratic organization has godlike dimensions; it dominates the earth. Like God, it exists everywhere and no human activity is free of its control. In contrast to the palaces of traditional and charismatic leaders, it lacks splendor and glory, but this only strengthens the sense of dominance. In his search for the Court of Inquiry, Joseph K. expects to find a building recognizable at a distance by a sign or by some unusual commotion before the door, but instead finds himself in a street with houses almost exactly alike on both sides, high gray tenements inhabited by poor people. The inquiry takes place in a setting we hardly associate with a court of law (although it fits quite accurately the actual location of courts in many cities of the world):

> [M]ost of the windows were occupied, men in shirt-sleeves were leaning there smoking or holding small children cautiously and tenderly on the window ledges. Other windows were piled high with bedding, above which the disheveled head of a woman would appear for a moment.[22]

Nor is there splendor and glory in the offices. In his exploration of the empty courtroom, K. finds "a long passage, a lobby communicating by ill-fitting doors with the different offices on the floor."²³ It is in such unimpressive offices that we rule ourselves in the age of the routinization of charisma; this is where the law is housed. At times we draw political leaders in a glorious fashion, as Titoreli, the painter, who was ordered to paint them, tells Joseph K.:

> 'You have painted the figure as it actually stands above the high seat.' 'No,' said the painter, 'I have neither seen the figure nor the high seat, that is all invention, but I am told what to paint and I paint it.'²⁴

Behind the judge, a large figure is drawn, with a bandage over her eyes and wings on her heels, the goddess of justice and the goddess of victory in one. That figure represents the end of political philosophy as it proclaims the ultimate combination of power and justice that has culminated in modern bureaucracy. The quest for a normative authority structure, which began with Trasymachus's claim that might is right, has been completed, as modern bureaucracy is both legal-rational and normative. Yet we are not allowed any illusions as to who the figures exercising that authority are. Facing a picture of a judge, possibly his judge, K. sees a man in a judge's robe seated on a high throne-like seat, but the judge does not appear in a dignified composure. Instead he appears in a violent and threatening position and we find out he is none other than a low-ranking official "sitting on a kitchen chair, with an old horse-rug doubled under him."²⁵

This, then, is the nature of the modern authority structure – a system of unimpressive clerks located in ugly offices whose routine activities disrupted by minute incidents represent "the law." As in the famous fable appearing in *The Trial* about the inability to enter the sphere of law, we are both exposed to and removed from the nature of modern authority. The authority structure is defined by the law – "you see, everything belongs to the Court"²⁶ Joseph K. is told – but its disruptions, being so minute, come as a surprise, and hence the organizational apparatus goes astray. And when this happens, the individual – not the organization – is the victim. As a lawyer informs K., there is no chance for individuals to reform the system because the individual is destructible while the system is not:

> One must lie low, no mater how much it went against the grain, and try to understand that this great organization remained, so to speak, in a state of delicate balance, and that if someone took it upon himself to alter the disposition of things around him, he ran the risk of losing his footing and falling to destruction, while the organization would simply right itself by some compensating reaction in another part of its machinery – since everything interlocked – and remain unchanged, unless, indeed, which was very probable, it became still more rigid, more vigilant, severer, and more ruthless.[27]

The ability of bureaucracy to remain intact stems from its total nature – it encompasses the public sphere *in toto* with no civil society to mediate between the individual and the organization and evaluate the normative behavior of both. The individual does not face the organization but is interlocked into its hierarchical bureaus. The book begins with Joseph K.'s arrest when he himself rings a bell that brings representatives of the law into his room, and it ends with his death inflicted by a bizarre cooperation between him and the two policemen killing him:

> In complete harmony all three now made their way across a bridge in the moonlight, the two men readily yielded to K.'s slightest movement, and when he turned slightly toward the parapet they turned, too, in a solid front.[28]

K. is not just subjected to organizational routines, he is part of them; when his uncle comes to visit from the country, he arrives at K.'s bank accompanied by two clerks bringing his nephew some papers to sign. In *The Trial* we find no domestic or social system – just bureaucratic routines. Not only are all individuals faceless, the disappearance of the private sphere is symbolized by such details as the smartness of the clerks' clothing. The court's clerk of inquiries is smartly dressed because the staff took up for him; to which some of the clients even contributed. In other words, the entire "social system" is mobilized. Sometimes an individual may grumble about the need to fulfill a role but the roles are always fulfilled.

This, of course, commands a heavy price that is not spelled out but is apparent on every page of the book. The merger of the individual and the organization, with no mediating social groups, leads to uncertainty and despair. Joseph K. is weak and helpless – when a student grabs the Examining Magistrate's wife he has an urge to play savior but both the woman and K. rationalize her captivity:

> 'And you don't want to be set free,' cried K., laying his hand on the shoulder of the student, who snapped at it with his teeth. 'No,' cried the woman pushing K. away with both hands. 'No, no, you mustn't do that, what are you thinking of? It would be the ruin of me. Let him alone, oh, please let him alone! He's only obeying the orders of the Examining Magistrate and carrying me to him.' 'Then let him go, and as for you, I never want to see you again.' Said K.[29]

The last sentence indicates a degree of frustration over the failure of the rescue operation through the victim's fault, but K. soon rationalizes it:

> There was no reason, of course, for him to worry about that, he had received the defeat only because he had insisted on giving battle. While he stayed quietly at home and went about his ordinary vocations he remained superior to all these people and could kick any of them out of his path.[30]

However K. rationalizes his condition, he is still miserable. Our exposure to the limited private sphere of one cog in the bureaucratic wheel may thus be seen as a call for a dialogue between individuals and the social groups mediating between them and the inevitable bureaucratic structures. Joseph K., facing the organization with no family, friends, or social and political support groups, is desperate. His world is sad and shallow, as symbolized by the view from his office window where one sees nothing but "a slice of empty housewall between two shop windows."[31]

Kafka, who suffered loneliness in the offices he worked in, did not assume an easy adjustment to the bureaucratic world. True, K. yields to that world in every respect ("he suffered the two of them to discuss him as if he were an inanimate object, indeed he actually preferred that"[32]) and may be seen as responsible in existentialist fashion for his condition, but his despair is hard to ignore:

> One winter morning-snow was falling outside the window in a foggy dimness – K. was sitting in his office, already exhausted in spite of the early hour. To save his face before his subordinates at least, he had given his clerk instructions to admit no one, on the plea that he was occupied with an important piece of work. But instead of working he twisted in his chair, idly rearranged the things lying on his writing-table, and then, without being aware of it, let his outstretched arm rest on the table and went on sitting motionless with bowed head.[33]

This desperate condition extends by far the traditional structure of bureaucracy. It can be attributed to organizational reality in less obvious settings than Prague of 1914. In *The Organization Man*, published in 1956, William Whyte has shown that individuals in the democratic United States rationalize no less than Joseph K. their servitude to the omnipotent structure of post World War II organizations:

> They are all, as they so often put it, in the same boat. Listen to them talk to each other over the front lawns of their suburbia and you cannot help but be struck by how well they grasp the common denominators which bind them. Whatever the differences in their organization ties, it is the common problems of collective work that dominate their attentions, and when the Du Pont man talks to the research chemist or the chemist to the army man, it is these problems that are uppermost. The word *collective* most of them can't bring themselves to use – except to describe foreign countries or organizations they don't work for – but they are keenly aware of how much more deeply beholden they are to organization than were their elders.[34]

Scholars studying human relations in organizations worked under the assumption that there need be no conflict between the individual and the organizational structure, but to Whyte there was such a conflict: "the peace of mind offered by organization remains a surrender, and no less so for being offered in benevolence."[35] In other words, while the material conditions and self-esteem of workers in organizations had improved since Kafka wrote *The Trial*, this improvement subordinated them even more to the organization. And the more individuals were given the illusion that the organizational structures they worked in were being replaced by more friendly ones, the more valid Joseph K.'s message had become.

In the 1960s it was widely believed that corporate cultures in the United States, Western Europe, and Japan had found the way to accommodate the individual in the organization. John Kenneth Galbraith's *The New Industrial State*, published in 1967, was a landmark in its optimism regarding the emancipated industrial system. The book described the decline of the traditional entrepreneur and the rise of a "technostructure" composed of those who bring specialized knowledge, talent, or experience to industrial organizations. Reflecting a common trend according to which knowledge was seen as liberating, Galbraith was hopeful:

> The industrial system, by making trained and educated manpower the decisive factor of production, requires a highly developed educational system. If the educational system serves generally the beliefs of the industrial system, the influence and monolithic character of the latter will be enhanced. By the same token, should it be superior to and independent of the industrial system, it can be the necessary force for skepticism, emancipation and pluralism.[36]

Yet Galbraith knew that such superiority and independence had a small chance. As he himself admitted, higher education at the time extensively accommodated to the needs of the industrial system, and it was hard to expect that, as it did so, critical thinking would prevail. There was no reason to expect that the rise of knowledge elites in modern industrial societies would have an emancipating effect if only because of the tendency by knowledge elites to justify the industrial system rather than to criticize it. When knowledge was harnessed to the tasks of the modern industrial state,

Knowledge w/o Skepticism

mainly during the Cold War, it lost the "skepticism, emancipation and pluralism" associated with it, and although university presidents never ceased to pay lip service to the liberal arts, knowledge was more associated with the conformity of the engineer than with the skepticism of the philosopher. Students prepared themselves to a life in the service of the modern industrial state by studying engineering, computer science, business administration, and law and were socialized into the modes of thought associated with these professions, which only rarely included Socratic skepticism.

No field of study was more popular than "management." In the second half of the twentieth century, the manager replaced the ideologue as the focus of human development and infinite studies of managerial techniques under such titles as " Who Moved My Cheese?" promised to improve the organizational setting in which the technological revolution of the twentieth century was steered. A managerial revolution was underway, reinforced by the enormous financial success in the eighties and nineties of high-tech companies operating in a new fashion. Until the collapse of Nasdaq, which marked the end of the illusion that high-tech companies represent an unbeatable economic domain, it seemed that a new era, nullifying Kafka's bureaucratic nightmares, had begun. That era was characterized by a restructuring of the workforce in line with the high-tech culture.

This included the seating of knowledge workers in open spaces while giving them a sense of worth and prominence inside and outside the organization, unprecedented channels of mobility, and skyrocketing financial rewards. It also included the substantial shortening of lines of command and control, organizational transparency, and the reformulation of organizational tasks in modular ways. The new organization, replacing the old-fashioned bureaucracy, was expected to adapt better to change, uncertainty, and complexity in the organization's environment and to cater to the value of individualism. Peter Drucker, one of the main advocates of the new, open, information-based organization, puts it as follows:

> In the traditional organization – the organization of the last one hundred years – the skeleton, or internal structure, was a combination of rank and power. In the emerging organization, it has to be mutual understanding and responsibility.[37]

The new organizational setting, however, did not avoid the Kafkaean malaise. Joseph K.'s uncertainty, loneliness, helplessness, and fear hardly disappeared. Like Whyte's suburbia, workers in high-tech companies may have lived in denial and rationalized their condition as divine, but Joseph K.'s warnings have not been nullified in the open spaces of IBM or Microsoft. To the contrary, some of the features of *The Trial* have only become more salient.

First, the workplace has not necessarily become more pleasant and joyful, considering the long hours of work required in the new organizations and the enormous effort it took to try and survive in a highly competitive job market. The mass media have often portrayed high-tech workers as joyful beings but, as is well known, the discrepancy between the ways one's life is portrayed in the media and how it looks in reality often leads to stress. The success of women in climbing the corporate ladder in the 1980s and 1990s, for instance, led to great stress over the need to match the superhuman qualities attributed to them in the media, especially when such qualities were actually needed to overcome the many obstacles involved. The open spaces and other characteristics of the new organizations of the late twentieth century did not help diminish the difficulties of individuals lacking job security and operating in an uncertain environment characterized by mergers and takeovers leading to mass layoffs.

Second, the condition of confinement to the organization has not changed. Paradoxically, the more uncertain knowledge workers became about their workplace, the more hours they had to invest, which amounted to feudal servitude. Corporations and their fellow travelers in the field of management presented the mobility opportunities of knowledge workers as never-ending, but insecurity over one's future, especially when a certain age had been reached which made competition in the knowledge-based industry extremely hard, filled many hearts with Kafkaean gloom.

Third, with the increasing complexity of the world, and the burgeoning role of the mass media in that world, the fundamental problem raised by Kafka over the subordination of the individual to gigantic structures conveying moral authority whose source and validity is unknown became only more severe. Late-twentieth-century men and women found themselves in a world moralizing its actions on every level: on the international level, where a new world order marked by a global human rights regime was said to emerge, on the national level, where political leaders equipped with daily polling results promised people everything they wanted to hear, and on the corporate level where a cruder than ever financial greed was covered, mainly in television commercials, by claims of transparency, community service, ecological concern, and the like. As a consequence, individuals lost every sense of right and wrong when it came to the organizational systems surrounding them. The political rhetoric of global NGOs became as void as that of national leaders, corporate CEOs, or military officers once the competition over the public sphere necessitated the recruitment of public relations firms.

When appearance becomes as important as substance, it is impossible to identify the sources of policies, to evaluate their costs and benefits, and get a sense of how sincere their advocates are. Indeed, every policy and activity was presented as normative. Late-twentieth-century Joseph K. was not just summoned to court (although many individuals were when human negotiations over such issues as doctor–patient relations have increasingly been replaced by lawsuits). The individual faced a gigantic network of self-righteous political, economic, military, and civil organizations demanding adherence to an unclear, unstable, transient ethics. The lack of a valid source of moral authority was apparent, for instance, when military intervention by the "international community" was conducted in some instances and refrained from in others, or when the same actions by politicians, corporate executives, or celebrities were praised one day and condemned on another day, when the mood in the media had changed.

Finally, Joseph K. has often been referred to when individuals complained about their entanglement in organizational systems claiming efficiency but turning life into a nightmare as a result of small disruptions. Those required to push buttons on their telephones in order to get a service but getting disconnected instead, those subjected to recordings telling them their business was important to someone who nevertheless kept them waiting for hours, or those who acquired the newest, most expensive computer only to find out it requires "upgrading," could easily identify with Kafka's character. That character conveyed the feeling of helplessness sensed by those who faced the dial phone button, the answering machine, or the computer world alone. The more "user-friendly" the world had allegedly become at the end of the century, and the more righteous the systems surrounding us, the more timely Joseph K.'s message about the need to maintain the diminishing domestic and social affiliations enabling us to preserve a degree of mental health and social civility.

In Quest of Authenticity

In *The Meaning of the Twentieth Century,* published in 1964, economist Kenneth Boulding spelled out the parameters of the great transition undergone by the human race in the twentieth century. He compared its power and intensity to the transition from pre-civilized to civilized societies five to ten thousand years ago. The first transition was based on agriculture; it was not until people settled down and began to cultivate crops and domesticate animals that a surplus of food developed which could sustain the kings, priests, soldiers, and artisans of urban civilization. The second transition is based on technology. While the first transition gave rise to the differences between cultures, Boulding claims, the technological transition leads to uniformity because its techniques are much less bound either to geography or to past culture than were the techniques of the past.[1]

The uniformity brought about by modern technology became a major theme in such writings as John Kenneth Galbraith's above-mentioned *The New Industrial State,* Jacques Ellul's *The Technological Society,* and Alvin

Toffler's *Future Shock*. Galbraith explained the imperatives of technology in the industrial process, especially the need for certainty, rationality, and long-range planning, and the rise of a technocratic class in modern industrial states committed to these values.[2] Ellul lamented the subordination of all social and cultural systems to technology, claiming that "when technique enters into every area of life, including the human, it ceases to be external to man and becomes his very substance."[3] And Toffler stressed the difficulty that individuals and social systems had in progressing with technology.[4]

Technology – the application of scientific means to industrial use – has always led to social, economic, and cultural change. The introduction of a tractor into a village that previously had no tractors changes property relations, family structures, the division of labor, economic expectations, demands for education, etc. What characterized twentieth-century technology, however, was its absolute effect; the changes brought about by technology were fast, interrelated, and overwhelming. The atomic bomb, antibiotics, the space program, radio, television, the car, the airplane, the pill, the personal computer, and many other products of technology changed all spheres of life and nowhere could their effects be avoided. So much so, that the technological revolution was seen as inevitable.

Although technology supposedly developed to benefit humankind, its wide-ranging effects raised deep concern. Charlie Chaplin's film *Modern Times* reflected the fear of many over the subordination of the individual to the machine. The age-old question "who governs?" was given new urgency. Once it was perceived that genetic engineering, for instance, would provide humanity with the means to change human qualities, the problem of who would be in charge of that process became more crucial than ever before. Democracy had a ready-made answer – it put its faith in the elect – but citizens of democracies were well aware that elected officials lacked the necessary expertise to follow complex processes like genetic engineering. And nobody was particularly eager to see those who did have the expertise – scientists – take control and serve as a "new priesthood."[5]

Brave New World is one of the main expressions of the fear of technology and its effects. Huxley, born in 1884 to a family of well-known scientists, hoped to become a medical doctor, but due to his poor eyesight had to give it up and became an essayist and novelist. *Brave New World*'s success may be partly attributed to the year of its publication: 1932. Like many others,

Huxley feared the rising force of fascism and described the future world as one of absolute control by the state over its citizens made possible by the power of the sciences, especially the life and behavioral sciences, to condition individuals into a state of total submission. In the world of the 1930s, which feared fascism and suspected science and technology, the book soon became a classic, side by side with *Frankenstein*, *Dr. Jekyll and Mr. Hyde*, and similar fiction.

One of the greatest fears of technology concerns its destruction of authentic life. "Authenticity" refers to a way of life that follows its presumed nature. Political theorists have debated for centuries what constitutes the "state of nature," but the very quest for it meant that cultural constructs were believed to have a natural base whose recognition is crucial to the normative ordering of these constructs, notably the state. In social contract theory, for instance, the development of the political state is explained by the natural conditions from which it emerged, and it is expected to behave in accordance with norms implied by these conditions. The technological revolution, however, was seen as bringing about new physical and cultural constructs that contradicted nature, e.g., a human habitat without fresh air or a state armed with weapons of mass destruction that denies its citizens their natural right, which lies at the core of social contract theory, to live in peace and safety.

Although Huxley's characters are insufficiently developed, John the Savage carries an important message: he represents an authentic existence in nature. *Brave New World* begins with a visit by a group of students to a hatchery and conditioning center in which they observe the artificial fertilizing and psychological conditioning of human beings. The center is located in a setting devoid of sunlight, seasonal change, or any other natural phenomena:

> The enormous room on the ground floor faced towards the north. Cold for all the summer beyond the panes, for all the tropical heat of the room itself, a harsh thin light glared through the windows, hungrily seeking some draped lay figure, some pallid shape of academic gooseflesh, but finding only the glass and nickel and bleakly shining porcelain of a laboratory.[6]

Literature, art, and folklore have long stressed the separation of urban life from nature, but only the technological revolution of the twentieth century has provided substitutes, such as this laboratory, in which nature is abandoned altogether. The laboratory workers are white, their hands gloved with a pale corpse-colored rubber, and the light is "frozen, dead, a ghost"[7] This is not the assembly line of the industrial revolution; it is a preview of the atomic shelters and space colonies that separate human beings from flowers, trees, and other natural phenomena. In the brave new world, babies are conditioned to hate books and roses. Primroses and landscapes have one grave defect: they are gratuitous, as a love of nature keeps no factories busy. In the brave new world, the love of nature is abolished.

In a forward added to *Brave New World* in 1946, the author regretted the strict dichotomy he had suggested a decade earlier between nature and technological civilization, but the book provides only two alternatives: "an insane life in Utopia, or the life of a primitive in an Indian village."[8] Contrary to the romantic view of nature advanced by thinkers like Rousseau, here the choice between nature and culture is not an easy one. In contrast to the inhabitants of utopia, John the Savage lives an authentic life but the Indian reserve is by no means a romantic place: "The place was queer, so was the music, so were the clothes and the goiters and the skin diseases and the old people."[9] Yet this natural setting provides an alternative to the technological civilization gone astray. It shatters this civilization's "commonplaces of progressive hopes for mankind"[10] and exposes "the irony inherent in the absolute success of a scientific-sociological vision."[11]

Huxley realizes that most humans are quite unwilling to tolerate the conditions on the Indian reserve and therefore will be prepared to sign a pact with the technological devil. History has been filled with insecurity, poverty, and pain while technology promises a world devoid of them. Who wouldn't be willing to give up his home and family, Huxley ironically asks, for a brave new world of laboratories, microscopes, and polished tubes in which babies are cloned:

> Home, home – a few small rooms, stiflingly overinhabited by a man, by a periodically teeming woman, by a rabble of boys and girls of all ages. No air, no space; an understerilized prison; darkness, disease, and smells ... a rabbit hole, a midden, hot

with the frictions of tightly packed life, reeking with emotion. What suffocating intimacies, what dangerous, insane, obscene relationships between the members of the family group![12]

The irony seems to be directed mainly at Freudianism in which human faults are blamed on family life. Since Freud, the world has been filled with parents causing suffering, abuse, and sublimation, all of which are abolished by behavioral manipulation in utopia. So is art, literature, independent thought, moral choice, even religion. The technological civilization is a pagan one because religion stems from human suffering while technology supposedly overcomes it and hence nullifies the belief in God.

But the price of technology is the abandonment of authenticity. John the Savage remains authentic because he maintains his distance from the technological civilization. He prefers internal restraints to external conditioning, he prays and is close to God, he gives up the products of the consumer society and feels grateful for the landscape outside the city's skyscrapers. He tries to escape to an enclave where nature hasn't yet been destroyed. He enjoys "the woods, the open stretches of heather and yellow gorse, the clumps of Scotch firs, the shining ponds with their overhanging birch trees, their water lilies, their beds of rushes …"[13] but soon realizes that this vision is subdued in a technological world. As he attempts to "escape further contamination by the filth of civilized life,"[14] he is confronted by the press corps, film makers, tourists, and other representatives of the new industrial state who are staring, laughing, clicking their cameras, throwing peanuts, and leaving nothing to its genuine and authentic self.

The agents of the technological civilization do not leave room for individual liberty and self-control over one's environment. *Brave New World* is a statement about the price paid by humanity as it advances – willingly – towards technological solutions to human problems. Although the brave new world resembles the assembly line of the nineteenth century more than the industrial process of the 1930s (nuclear energy, for example, is not even mentioned), it provides a frame of reference for individuals who participate in the technological project yet realize the Faustian pact it involves, for technology implies the loss of authenticity.

Technology also implies the loss of democratic order. According to Huxley, it does not really matter whether technology is used by a fascist, communist, or liberal regime; the power to clone and condition human beings is equally frightening when it is given to an authoritarian elite or to some unidentified group. In this novel, national boundaries are broken, which leaves the impression that the technological process is controlled by an international elite whose motives and ideology remain unclear.

The students visiting the hatchery are confronted by Mustapha Mond, one of the world's ten controllers, who articulates the ideology of the brave new world. He conceives technology to be the central force in a civilization whose main value is the stability of the production process. Industrialization requires social stability that allows a steady flow of workers for the production process. Individuals have to be conditioned to fulfill their roles in that process, and the process must be tightly controlled so as to avoid a population explosion that would cause massive deaths once industry would not be able to feed the masses. Here is Mond speaking in six hundred years:

> The machine turns, turns and must keep on turning – for ever. It is death if it stands still. A thousand millions scrabbled the crust of the earth. The wheels began to turn. In a hundred and fifty years there were two thousand millions. Stop all the wheels. In a hundred and fifty weeks there are once more only a thousand millions; a thousand thousand thousand men and women have starved to death.
>
> Wheels must turn steadily, but cannot turn untended. There must be men to tend them, men as steady as the wheels upon their axles, sane men, obedient men, stable in contentment.[15]

The nature of the ruling elite remains unclear but not its inhuman character. It has abandoned those behaviors that characterized individuals in the past, such as care for the young and elderly:

> Crying: My baby, my mother, my only, only love; groaning: My sin, my terrible God; screaming with pain, muttering with fever, bemoaning old age and poverty – how can they tend the wheels?[16]

The brave new world is rational, well-organized (or rather over-organized) and lacks political choice. The ruling elites become unpredictable because they no longer rely merely on traditional means of power-acquisition but rather on scientific knowledge. The demise of brute force as the source of power becomes apparent in a series of fragments: "Government's an affair of sitting, not hitting. You rule with the brains and the buttocks, never with the fists."[17] The world controllers of the emerging future realize that force is no good in comparison to slower but infinitely surer methods such as neo-Pavlovian conditioning. This transforms government from a political institution born in force and thus overthrown by force if necessary to a faceless creature that lasts forever. The government is totalitarian; it includes such institutions as bureaus of propaganda, a college of emotional engineering, press offices, and research laboratories, all of which assure the government's eternity.

The government intervenes in the most intimate processes of life. It controls no less than hormone injection, artificial dissemination, abortion, natural birth, breast-feeding, and similar matters mainly concerning the woman's body. This is frightening not only because of the brutality involved but because of the wide reach of the government. It is not only in charge of adapting humans to their industrial roles but also intervenes in the natural process of giving birth. As Huxley explains in a later essay:

> In the Brave New World of my fable socially desirable behaviour was ensured by a double process of genetic manipulation and post-natal conditioning. Babies were cultivated in bottles and a high degree of uniformity in the human product was assured by using ova from a limited number of mothers and by treating each ovum in such a way that it would split and split again, producing identical twins in batches of a hundred or more. In this way it was possible to produce standardized machine-minders for standardized machines.[18]

In that essay, Huxley admitted that the genetic standardization of individuals was still beyond human reach, but he warned that big government and big business already possessed, or were expected to possess soon, techniques that would allow mind manipulation. Lacking the ability to impose genetic uniformity upon embryos, he believed, the rulers of tomorrow's overpopulated and over-organized world would try to impose social and cultural uniformity upon adults and their children. If this kind of tyranny is to be avoided, he contended, we must begin without delay to educate ourselves and our children for freedom and self-government.

What chance is there to educate the masses participating in the technological project to recognize its dangers and fight against them? This task is made rather hard by the mass drugging of the population in the technological age. In an essay titled "Chemical Persuasion," Huxley explained the wide use of a drug named Soma in his utopia:

> In the Brave New World the Soma habit was not a private vice; it was a political institution, it was the very essence of the Life, Liberty and Pursuit of Happiness guaranteed by the Bill of Rights. But this most precious of the subjects' inalienable privileges was at the same time one of the most powerful instruments of rule in the dictator's armoury. The systematic drugging of individuals for the benefit of the State (and incidentally, of course, for their delight) was a main plank in the policy of the World Controllers.[19]

Technology makes it possible for the masses to engage in hedonism; a much larger percentage of the population in the twentieth century was offered the means to enjoy the pleasures previously reserved for the nobility. The hedonistic culture, however, is disturbing to Huxley because hedonism is inconsistent with freedom. Like drug addicts, individuals consume the products and images of a society that promises happiness but allows a political elite to manipulate the population.

The problem of drugs, television, free sex, and other means to entertain whole populations to death is articulated in *Brave New World* by Bernard Marx. Marx is deformed as a result of alcohol mixed in his blood and hence conscious of the traditional values lost in the excessive pursuit of happiness. As a result of his deformity, he does not respond properly to his conditioning in the brave new world and thus objects to leisure activities conducted in public. He invites "Lenina," who is well adjusted to the new world, to take a walk with him for a couple of hours and talk, but she fails to understand the value of talking and prefers to fly, in jet-set fashion, to Amsterdam to join a crowd watching the "Semi-Demi Finals of the Women's Heavyweight

Wrestling Championship." Bernard's reaction: "I'd rather be myself ... myself and nasty. Not somebody else, however jolly."[20] In other words, happiness is identified here with the loss of one's self-identity. Lenina repeats clichés she was conditioned to absorb in her sleep, which make her appreciate the superficial joy provided by drugs and other means of gaining pleasure.

The endless pursuit of pleasures in modern industrial states is one of the reasons for the loss of authenticity. The deformed Bernard is capable of appreciating nature while Lenina uses electronic devices to hide from it. When Bernard pays attention to the rushing emptiness of the night, the black foam-flecked water, the pale face of the moon and the hastening clouds she prefers to turn on the radio. The political implications are clear. Bernard's capacity to appreciate nature is associated with individualism as opposed to becoming a cell in the social body. Lenina's enslavement to technology, on the other hand, is unconscious and appears under a pretence of freedom:

> 'Don't you wish you were free, Lenina?'
> 'I don't know what you mean. I am free. Free to have the most wonderful time. Everybody is happy nowadays.'
> He laughed, 'Yes. Everybody's happy nowadays. We begin giving the children that at five. But wouldn't you like to be free to be happy in some other way, Lenina? In your own way, for example; not in everybody else's way.'
> 'I don't know what you mean,' She repeated.[21]

Lenina's pursuit of pleasure, which Huxley associates with American society, seems to Bernard Marx a childish, unbalanced approach to life. But the ruling elite discourages a more mature approach because of the political advantages it gains when the population indulges in leisure activities. This is one of the strong meeting points between fascist and democratic regimes; the latter follows the former in the use of means that drug the masses. The "Semi-Demi Finals of the Women's Heavyweight Wrestling Championship" do not differ greatly from the fascist rallies and parades of the 1930s. In both cases, the population's attention is diverted from personal problems to public pleasures. Consider the singing and dancing in the brave new world as a means of enhancing solidarity in fascist fashion:

> Round they went, a circular procession of dancers, each with hands on the hips of the dancer preceding, round and round, shouting in unison, stamping to the rhythm of the music with their feet, beating it, beating it out with hands on the buttocks in front; twelve pairs of hands beating as one; twelve buttocks slabbily resounding.[22]

This novel's contribution to the civil society model, then, lies in its emphasis on authenticity. The political demands for life, liberty, and the pursuit of happiness, conceived as natural rights, are replaced by the horrors of a technological society controlled by anonymous forces. The contribution is somewhat limited as a result of the novel's strict polarization between the life in a brave new world made of glass and aluminum structures vs. the life of John the Savage which involves a total return to nature. It is limited because the new industrial state has shown greater consciousness about natural and ecological considerations than Huxley expected, especially after the student revolts of the 1960s. Huxley was versed in the scientific literature of his time but failed to understand the various options open to the modern industrial state; *Brave New World* always remained a statement by those fearing it in an abstract sense.[23]

The book expresses the ideology of a declining British aristocracy feeling threatened by technological development. For instance, Huxley did not think beyond the English class system. It is unclear why the industrial state six hundred years into the future should resemble that system in its encouragement of class-consciousness among children or why the differentiation between classes would be part of the industrial process of the future. At one point, a classless society is mentioned when Huxley tells of an experiment in future Cyprus in which all agricultural and industrial functions were left to one class. The results "fulfilled all the theoretical predictions,"[24] namely, that the system wouldn't work because all the people detailed to a shift at low-grade work were constantly intriguing to obtain high-grade jobs, and all the people with high-grade jobs were counter-intriguing at all costs to stay where they were.

This, of course, is a prediction based not on essential conditions of the new industrial state but on the novelist's own prejudices. The distinction between "high-grade" and "low-grade" jobs may easily blur in the future, as shown in many corporations. Huxley was obviously influenced by scientific management theories intended to increase the productivity of industrial workers. But in 1932, these theories were no longer the last word in the field, and theories stressing the importance of human relations in the industrial process, intended to reduce the frustration and alienation of "low grade" workers, were already prevalent.

Huxley issued a warning about the dangers awaiting us once science and technology are controlled by dark forces. The atrocious use of science and technology in World War II has validated these warnings and turned Huxley into a prophet of doom. It must be recalled however, that the Allies in winning World War II also used science and technology. As destructive as technologies can be, they can also be used for the construction of a better world. A utopia looking six hundred years into the future cannot assume a one-dimensional path. Just as the modern industrial state can censor books and flowers, it can provide the masses with access to books and the leisure time to read them. In *Brave New World*, children are ugly, uniform, conditioned creatures but modern science and technology have liberated many children from slavery, provided them with open education, and, without sending them to an Indian reserve, have constructed – through the distribution of computers, for example – a private sphere that allows them to develop as free and enlightened individuals.

In one fragment the author reveals his main objection to the modern industrial state; he objects to its effectiveness. The essence of liberalism is defined as the right to be ineffective:

> Sleep teaching was actually prohibited in England. There was something called liberalism. Parliament, if you know what that was, passed a law against it. The records survive. Speeches about liberty of the subject. Liberty to be inefficient and miserable. Freedom to be a round peg in a square hole.[25]

As the twentieth century came to a close, however, it was not the efficiency of the new industrial state that was worrisome but its inefficiency; flaws of the kind discussed by Kafka threatened to turn it into a nightmare. The human ability to uncover the genetic code or to engineer behavior became less perturbing than such occurrences as the transplant of organs to a teenager who died because the blood type of the donor had not been properly checked. Such apparently small disruptions in the system threatened the entire technological project because they exposed the discrepancy between the ambitions of the human race and its actual capabilities. The organizational order within which governments, militaries, industries, hospitals, schools, police departments, and other institutions operated did not adjust to the demands of complex technological projects. Attempts to reorganize in accordance with these demands, e.g., the establishment of NASA in the late 1950s or the introduction of rational planning, programming, budgeting processes in the U.S. Department of Defense in the 1960s were presented as success stories until the truth about human rivalries, character deficiencies, or what Barabara Tuchman saw as sheer folly became apparent.[26]

Moreover, a whole culture of cover-up developed, in which political malfunction, military failures, medical negligence, environmental destruction, leaks in nuclear reactors, and other disasters were either hidden from the public eye or blurred when revealed. The cover-up culture that developed in all spheres of the modern industrial state threatened the entire industrial project because it stood in contrast to the norms of sincerity, transparency, and information-sharing that made the project possible in the first place. Political leaders and industrial managers could perhaps be expected to engage in cover-ups, especially after the Watergate affair, which revealed the magnitude of the phenomenon, but doctors, engineers, programmers, and other professionals, threatened by just and unjust accusations for their role in the execution of flawed technological ventures, were also found very often to transform their professional mode of thinking into a public relations orientation. The joke that professionals no longer make a move without a lawyer became reality.

Rather than turning into the hedonistic monster foreseen by Huxley, the United States at the end of the twentieth century resembled more a clumsy Middle Ages knight. American scholars have celebrated their country's victory in the Cold War against the Soviet Union by the supremacy of American technology – especially by the success of President Ronald Reagan's ambitious "Star Wars" program – and were partly right. In contrast to the corrupt Soviet Union, the U.S. succeeded in turning the electric circuit, the semiconductor, the microchip, and other inventions into products of political and military might without impoverishing society. At the end of the twentieth century, many Americans and other Westerners enjoyed warm houses, cheap automobiles, reasonable air-travel, color TVs, banking machines, personal computers, and other products of technology. The drive to export these products to consumers all over the world brought about the notion of "globalization," referring among other things to world hegemony of American technology.

The success story of American technology had, however, three loopholes. First, at the end of the century it became harder and harder to ignore the fact that disasters, from the sinking of the Titanic in 1912 to the destruction of the Challenger space shuttle in 1986, are not just "accidents" but an imminent part of life in a world dependent on technology. Second, it became clear that technological supremacy is a necessary but not a sufficient condition of national success. American foreign and security policy, highly dependent on technology, was often unsuccessful, as demonstrated in the failure to win the Vietnam War, the collapse of operation "Eagle Claw" intended to rescue American hostages from Iran in 1979, or the failure of American Patriot missiles to shoot down even one Iraqi Scud during the Gulf War of 1991. And third, it became more and more obvious that technology entails dangerous social side effects. Wade Rowland summarizes this point as follows:

> The negative side to all this "progress" is too well known to bear much discussion: the depredations of the automobile, for instance, are many and well understood. The daily toll in traffic fatalities alone would have stunned the most jaded nineteenth-century industrialist. Television's damage to the social fabric seems indisputable, if unquantifiable. That the social costs of modern technologies have been, on occasion, great, is beyond argument.[27]

Thus, as the twentieth century came to a close, neither the U.S. nor any other country had to worry about over-effectiveness. The liberty to be inefficient and miserable sought by Huxley was hardly endangered, and there was plenty of freedom "to be a round peg in a square hole." The main danger to liberty, as demonstrated on September 11, 2001, came not from the champions of technology but from fundamentalist forces skilled in using the products of technology to weaken Western democracies. On September 11, Huxley's challenge to maintain authenticity within the confines of the modern industrial state paled in comparison to the new challenge faced by the world's democracies to defend themselves against those who, in the name of an anti-technological ideology, seemed determined to destroy civility altogether.

Resisting Big Brother

During the Cold War it was customary to discuss Nazi Germany, Stalinist Russia, and other dictatorships under the heading of "totalitarianism."[1] This term was defined as the subordination of whole societies to the control of single political parties and was considered part of the malaise of modernity by Hannah Arendt,[2] Carl Friedrich,[3] Jacob Talmon,[4] and other analysts who were both horrified and fascinated by its vitality.

George Orwell's *1984*, published in 1948, became a major literary expression of the totalitarian phenomenon. Its publication at the beginning of the Cold War led to its consideration in the West as an account of life in Stalinist Russia: "big brother" reflected the cult of personality, "doublethink" the use of systemic lies, and the "two minutes of hate," the diversion of attention from the regime's troubles to internal or external enemies.[5] In the year 1984, many symposia were held in which *1984* served as a standard by which democratic societies measured their closeness or remoteness from the totalitarian phenomenon.[6]

Here, I would like to take a post-Cold-War perspective and suggest that Orwell's negative utopia, and the warnings conveyed by its main character, Winston Smith, could be seen as addressed at all twentieth-century political systems, not only those defined as totalitarian. I do not refer to the common argument that Orwell issued a warning to the democratic states they may turn totalitarian. I claim that the book can be read as a political pamphlet about "politics as usual." *1984* is a book about power in any state written by an intellectual who understood its meaning in the fullest sense.

Orwell's insights into the nature and effects of power could be partly attributed to his life story. He was born in 1903 as Arthur Eric Blaire, the son of an official of the British administration in Bengal. After graduating from various boarding schools, he served in the imperial police in Burma. As he writes in his memoirs, this experience taught him the meaning of authority; in observing an execution he internalized, for instance, what it means to take a human life. In his short story "Shooting an Elephant," relating to his days in Burma, inner knowledge of the colonial experience was demonstrated.

Orwell became a moderate socialist, expounding in his writings the cause of the working classes, and volunteered to fight in the Spanish Civil War where he was badly injured. His experience in Spain taught him of the deceit practiced by the Soviet Union, and his service in the BBC during World War II further taught him that all societies employ deceit.[7] In his two celebrated novels *Animal Farm* and *1984* he did not leave much hope for the democratic world.

Particularly pessimistic is the scene in *1984* in which party official O'Brien, representing crude totalitarianism, holds a lengthy conversation with Winston Smith while torturing him. The latter's feeling that a whole civilization could not be based on fear, hatred, and cruelty is dismissed by O'Brien, who knows that all the norms that could restrain the evil mind had been lost. Winston brings up his belief in human nature and claims it would be outraged by totalitarianism and turn against it, but O'Brien reminds him that the regime creates human nature. Nor does Kantian humanism bear any hope because it lost its validity with the death of God:

> 'There is something in the universe – I don't know, some spirit, some principle – that you will never overcome'
> 'Do you believe in God, Winston?'

'No'
'Then what is it, this principle that will defeat us?'
'I don't know. The spirit of Man'
'And you consider yourself a man?'
'Yes'
'If you are a man, Winston, you are the last man. Your kind is extinct ...'[8]

It is hard to believe that just two decades ago these lines on the extinction of humanism were attributed to totalitarian regimes or, when applied to democratic regimes, were merely seen as a warning, not a reflection of life in a democracy. During the Cold War, analysts were reluctant to apply Orwell's negative utopia directly to Western democracies. There are of course major differences between totalitarian and democratic states. Human rights, the rule of law, freedom of expression, and other democratic norms and practices are invaluable and citizenship in a free country cannot be compared to life in a totalitarian dictatorship. However, twentieth-century democracies have also witnessed the demise of those ethical principles that allowed individuals to resist the fear, hatred, and cruelty found in all political regimes.

The tortured Winston who lost the ethical base of resistance speaks for many inhabitants of democratic states. The lack of civility stemming from the demise of the norms that brought it into being applies both to the case of totalitarianism and to "politics as usual." *1984* is as much a book about London of 1948 as about Russia under Stalin or Germany under Hitler. The totalitarian insinuations add to the drama, but Winston Smith may be seen as an individual facing politics, any politics.

On the first page of the book we are introduced to Winston Smith who is thirty-nine years old and walks slowly because he has a varicose ulcer above his right ankle. At the end of the book, after his dramatic encounters with the state, he still remains the same person: "I'm thirty-nine years old. I've got a wife that I can't get rid of. I've got varicose veins. I've got false teeth."[9] Winston lives in a totalitarian state that provides "victory gin" in the workplace. As an ordinary person, he is more concerned with the burning he feels in his belly as a result of drinking that cheap gin than with its silly label. Therefore, like most ordinary persons, he is mainly confused by the political communications around him, which do not make much sense but cannot be ignored either. He is exposed to messages and images, such as that of a lifeboat full of children with a helicopter hovering over it, which, in his mind, turn into a "stream of rubbish."[10] Winston Smith assumes someone is probably making sense of it all, but he does not.

The difficulty to make sense of the political information in the surroundings is not unique to residents of totalitarian regimes. On any given day, citizens of the world's democracies have access to more information than they could absorb in a lifetime. Here are just the headlines of the CNN website on the day in which these lines are written (7 February 2003). They resemble no less a "stream of rubbish" if only for their sheer quantity.

The website includes a "breaking news" section announcing that "Terror Threat 'High.'" The word "high" appears in quotation marks, which raises immediately doubts as to whether the threat is really high or whether it had only been presented as such by some government official. Three government officials in black suits are shown near the Republic's flag in a photograph. The website produces terrifying information, which is particularly terrifying because very few readers can do anything about it. "For only the second time ever, the U.S. has raised the national terror threat level from 'elevated' to 'high,'" a headline says.

The rising of the threat level was allegedly done because of threats to hotels, apartment buildings, and other "soft" targets, yet, those living in these soft targets can hardly prepare for the unspecified threats. They can only assume, after Winston Smith, that the government officials in the photograph had a good reason to make the announcement. The website also tells the reader that the warnings issued to them were based on "specific intelligence," and that "fear of chem-bio attack grows." The fear can be assumed to grow if only because "chem-bio" sounds much more scary than "chemical biological."

These headlines are accompanied by "top stories" about shuttle Columbia's wing damage, a snow emergency in D.C., a slower than expected jobless rate, readiness of the nation for any North Korean contingencies, the expression of hope by a former president that Saddam Hussein will "come to his senses," and many other headlines concerning technological business and entertainment news of questionable relevance to most individuals faced by the information, e.g., "New 'Potter' to sell for record price."

With an overflow of information, citizens turn apathetic. Apathy is embodied in *1984* in the character of Julia, who couldn't care less if the party did or did not invent airplanes. Winston Smith spends a frustrating quarter of an hour arguing with her over it, getting annoyed when she does not even notice that the name of her country's enemy had changed, but why should it matter? Julia's response is typical of citizens faced with information that makes no sense because it is not placed within relevant categories:

> 'Who cares?' she said impatiently, 'it's always one bloody war after another, and one knows the news is all lies anyway…. She became bored and confused and said that she never paid any attention to that kind of thing. One knew that it was all rubbish, so why let oneself be worried about it?'[11]

Public opinion polls indicate that this approach to politics is quite common. Individuals are mainly ambivalent about the discrepancy between their bond to the regime they belong to and their realization that most of the time the regime is not concerned with their well-being. Winston Smith reflects that ambivalence when he participates in the hideous ecstasy of fear and vindictiveness organized by the regime in the two minutes of hate against its enemy. He participates in the hate scene even though his heart goes out to the lonely, derided addressee of the two minutes of hate, and he knows that his rage is "an abstract."[12] This ceremony is taken from the world of totalitarianism, but Winston Smith speaks for all citizens who feel that the political rhetoric addressed at them is not genuine and that the policies they help execute by nature of their political participation may be wrong.

Frustrated over his participation in the self-hypnotic acts demanded in the political process, Winston Smith writes on paper in large neat capital letters "down with big brother." In this quiet rebellion he reflects the frustration democratic citizens often feel towards institutions, such as the internal revenue service, which are ever-present in their lives. Citizens in democracies are not immune from the feeling that "the Thought Police would get him just the same,"[13] because they are no less guilty of the thought crime committed by Winston Smith. It is the crime of feeling in one's bones that despite one's participation in the ceremonies and rituals of politics, e.g., allowing candidates who couldn't care less about their well-being to shake their hands during election campaigns, something deep down in the political association between individuals is wrong.

This feeling stems from a fundamental problem built into any political system: its need for cognitive and emotional submission that is hard to achieve even after endless efforts at civic education. Even when they believe that their submission to the rules of the state is contractual, individuals are reluctant to give up their natural liberty. Orwell considers politics a maturation process in which we are torn from "a time when there were still privacy, love, and friendship, and when the members of a family stood by one another without needing to know the reason."[14] The political association is an abstract entity composed of individuals who find it difficult to relate to its abstract nature and may thus be accused of "thought crimes." They may be willing, in principle, to pay taxes to the state but feel differently about it the moment they have to put the check in the mail. Therefore, Orwell touches upon a hidden nerve when he describes the individual's constant fear of a knock on the door. Like Kafka, he was aware that even the most innocent citizen may expect a knock on the door, and like Kafka he realized that the worse thing of all is its delay, often for a whole lifetime.

The knock on the door has become so much a symbol of totalitarianism that it is hard to associate it with life in a democracy, but democratic citizens are also often preoccupied as taxpayers, drivers, or pot smokers with ways to avoid punishment by the state. States differ, of course, in many ways – the banners, processions, slogans, games, and community hikes are never the same, nor is the degree of freedom allowed the individual and the severity of punishment inflicted for violations of the law. But citizens everywhere have no way to obey all the laws, hence the universal preoccupation with ways to survive in the state. One need not live in Stalinist Russia in order to recognize the following insights:

> If you kept the small rules you could break the big ones.... The clever thing was to break the rules and stay alive all the same ... accepting the Party as something unalterable, like the sky, not rebelling against its authority but simply evading it, as a rabbit dodges a dog.[15]

There are always those who take part in the political process more enthusiastically than others, but in this novel there is no fundamental difference between the two types; government officials in *1984* do not seem much different from ordinary citizens. Party official O'Brien, a large, burly man with a thick neck and a coarse, humorous, brutal face, who evokes a momentary hush when he passes by, is fully integrated into the political system but does not look like a monster To the contrary, like many politicians, he possesses a certain charm of manner, and Winston Smith even trusts him. It is the trust often displayed vis-à-vis teachers, school principals, drill sergeants, bosses in the workplace, judges, and political officials who are feared and respected at the same time. O'Brien "had a trick of resettling his spectacles on his nose which was curiously disarming – in some indefinable way, curiously civilized."[16] Paradoxically, he continues to look civilized throughout the book because he is part of a culture that respects officials "that you could talk to."[17] This culture is not confined to totalitarian regimes but to every political setting in which some people are dependent on others who make decisions that affect their lives.

Another figure, Tom Parsons, represents the ultimate government official on whom the stability of the regime depends, but when we meet him in his home, he also does not look different from any ordinary person: his wife, for example, is preoccupied with a clot of human hair blocking up a water pipe. Other officials are no less ordinary:

> It was curious how that beetlelike type proliferated in the Ministries: little dumpy men, growing stout very early in life, with short legs, swift scuttling movements, and fat inscrutable faces with very small eyes.[18]

The fact that those who constitute the backbones of the political regime seem ordinary does not mean they do not possess great power. On the contrary, Winston Smith realizes that the Tom Parsons of the world will never be vaporized like the rest of us. They will last forever because no political system can do without the eyeless creature with the quacking voice that scuttles so nimbly through the labyrinthine corridors of power.

This is not to say that political recruitment in democratic and totalitarian regimes is the same and that political behaviors in free and dictatorial political systems do not differ in many ways. It may be said, however, that Orwell's negative utopia is quite reflective of the contemporary world whose efforts at democratization do not diminish many of the ills underlying the world of *1984*. I would like to emphasize three such ills we live with in the present: the rise of a technocratic elite, the omnipotence of the mass media, and the loss of historical memory.

A technocratic elite is one using the products of technology without commitment to any norms beyond the endurance of technology itself. This is why many technological developments with a potential to benefit the human race are met with fear. Whatever its potential benefits, technology becomes scary when the elites controlling it are not committed to civility. We refer to techniques as "Orwellian" not so much when those in control are evil but when they remain faceless. This is when techniques such as computerized files holding information about our private affairs, cameras monitoring our activities at work or during our leisure time, orbiting satellites reading our car's license plates, or means of wiretapping our telephone calls and e-mails frighten us the most.

The danger stems mainly from the rise of a new class of technocrats whose interest in the applications of technology is smaller than its interest in its development. Observers have often considered the rise of technocracy in the post World War II world as a blessing, but Orwell highlighted the dangers stemming from its interest in maintaining its power:

> The new aristocracy was made up for the most part of bureaucrats, scientists, technicians, trade-union organizers, publicity experts, sociologists, teachers, journalists, and professional politicians. These people, whose origins lay in the salaried middle class and the upper grades of the working class, had been shaped and brought together by the barren world of monopoly industry and centralized government. As compared with their opposite numbers in past ages, they were less avaricious, less tempted by luxury, hungrier for pure power, and, above all, more conscious of what they were doing and more intent on crushing opposition.[19]

Obviously, the methods used to crush opposition differ from one regime to the other, but the above paragraph refers to a familiar process in which technical means and a sheer hunger for power determine policy rather than any consistent value system. When values are either non-existent or serve as a disguise for power, the new class of technocrats becomes a threat. Once technology is used to perpetuate itself, or the power of its holders, be they scientists or politicians, democratic politics loses its meaning.

A second feature developed in *1984* that we live with in the present is the power of the mass media. Thomas Cooper has pointed at six components of what he called "Media Fascism"[20] foreseen in the book. These include the abolition of pluralism by a homogenizing mass media, the rise of television figures such as Walter Cronkite to positions of mental authority, the subjection of individuals to one-sided communication, the suppression of non-conformism, the restriction of language to appropriate thought forms, and the destruction of truth, reality, integrity, human dignity, and individual purpose. Towards the end of the twentieth century, these components seemed less threatening with the greater choice individuals got over the media they consume, especially with the introduction of cable TV, the VCR, and DVD and the Internet. With greater choice over channels, with the spread of interactive media and the endless opportunities at individual development opened by the Internet, the mass media could no longer be easily described as "big brother." Where Orwell's relevance remained, however, and even increased compared to the early years of the Cold War, was in the insights he proposed on the very presence of media in a person's life. However pluralistic the media, the subjection of individuals to hours of television watching or Internet surfing takes its toll, especially in the detachment from reality caused by the media.

The society Winston Smith lives in is a mass society in which the image of "big brother" is encountered everywhere: "on coins, on stamps, on the cover of books, on banners, on posters, and on the wrapping of a cigarette packet – everywhere."[21] But one image need not be so dominant in order for individuals to be controlled by images. As a result of the lack of means of surveillance, says Orwell in *1984*, all the tyrannies of the past were half-hearted and their ruling groups were infected to some extent by liberal ideas – even the Catholic Church of the Middle Ages was tolerant by modern standards. With the invention of print, however, it became easier to manipulate public opinion. Film and radio carried the process further, and with television private life came to an end.

Orwell understood the pacifying power of written and electronic media whose main feature is their constant presence. In a house in which the TV set is on for many hours, the endless images drown out human energy and creativity. It is not just the information transmitted by the media but the very fact that it is transmitted in large quantities that assures political control. Whether it stems from totalitarian intentions, or from commercial interests in capitalistic societies, the penetration of mostly useless data into the minds of individuals turns the latter into submissive objects. Orwell exposed the horror implied by the very magnitude of information. When Winston Smith engages in the manipulation of government data in the ministry of truth (in charge of lying) it is not just the lies that stand out but the activity itself which reveals the entire flow of information in society to be nothing but the substitution of one piece of nonsense for another. The following paragraph may be seen as a comment on the modern mass media:

> Most of the material that you were dealing with had no connection with anything in the real world, not even the kind of connection that is contained in a direct lie.[22]

The press in *1984* is described as rubbish newspapers, containing almost nothing except sport, crime, and astrology, sensational five-cent novelettes, films oozing with sex, and sentimental songs. The subjects of Orwell's negative utopia are overwhelmed by telescreens bruising everyone's ears with statistics proving that people live longer, work shorter hours, and are bigger, healthier, stronger, happier, more intelligent, and better educated than the people of fifty years ago. This description can be easily applied to present-day newspapers, radio, and TV channels using similar rhetoric to sell products and dreams. And although the Internet was expected to provide individuals with more choice over content, Internet providers were so far quite skillful in forcing users to face lots of trivial material in their surfing. Internet surfers are familiar with little boxes filled with ads, cartoons, technical warnings, and other unwanted information popping up. While the Internet has given us amazingly fast and effective access to data, it has also made us consumers of much useless and undesired information we encounter in its majestic world.

It may seem paradoxical to consider the Internet, which opens up to so many possibilities, as an Orwellian telescreen, but if we consider the relationship established by Orwell between excessive communication and control, the Internet cannot be excluded. In the last decade of the twentieth century, millions began to engage in online communication giving them the feeling of contact with other individuals. Online opinion sharing, love making or chess playing allowed people to bridge distances and avoid loneliness. They made new acquaintances, shared ideas, downloaded music, and received news. However, the Internet is also related to two phenomena that potentially subject individuals to political control: addiction and alienation.

Internet addiction, as part of more general computer addiction, has been described as a pathological disorder consisting of craving or compulsion, loss of control, and persistence that can't be helped despite its adverse consequences, such as the neglect of family life.[23] Millions of individuals found themselves thinking about their computer, obsessively checking their e-mail, or spending long nights in chat rooms – pathological behaviors resulting, like gambling or alcohol addiction, in apathy, anger, and fatigue, which can be easily exploited by powers providing the missing stimulation. A night spent in a chat room may be exciting but also alienating because the entire experience is mostly conducted in physical seclusion and involves a great potential of deceit. The human alienation involved is quite unclear yet, but it definitely requires consideration. So does the new phenomenon of "blogs," online diaries followed daily by thousands of surfers who have been found to turn to their favorite bloggers as main sources of political information in time of crisis and war,[24] which also involves a great potential of political control.

The third Orwellian feature relevant to today's world is the loss of memory, which is the main source of political control in *1984* and involves, in my opinion, the most important message conveyed by Winston Smith. By describing a political regime that destroys historical memory as a means to terrorize a population, Orwell brought to light the political implications of historical amnesia in today's world. In this regard, he may be seen as a prophet of post-modernism. Post-modernism is the contemporary intellectual trend, prevailing mainly in universities, according to which the memory of solid historical facts is mistrusted.[25]

Pauline Marie Rosenau associates this trend with the abandonment of four beliefs:

1. That there is a real, knowable past;
2. That historians should be objective;
3. That reason enables historians to explain the past; and
4. That the role of history is to transmit human, cultural and intellectual heritage from generation to generation.[26]

Rosenau shows how these beliefs are dismissed in a post-modern age in which history is viewed as egocentric, a source of myth, ideology, and prejudice, a creation of modern Western nations that oppresses other cultures.

In a book entitled *The Killing of History*, Keith Windschuttle accuses literary critics and social theorists of murdering the past. For thousands of years, he claims, history was associated with telling the truth, with the description of what really happened. Many historians were mistaken, but the discourse between them and their critics considered the match between historical statements and reality. The assumption prevailed that the truth was within the historian's grasp, while towards the end of the twentieth century, this assumption had been rejected:

> In the 1990s, the newly dominant theorists within the humanities and social sciences assert that it is impossible to tell the truth about the past or to use history to produce knowledge in any objective sense at all. They claim we can only see the past through the perspective of our own culture and, hence, what we see in history are our own interests and concerns reflected back at us. The central point upon which history was founded no longer holds: there is no fundamental distinction any more between history and myth.[27]

Once there is no longer a past, then control, according to Orwell, is assured: "If both the past and the external world exist only in the mind, and if the mind itself is controllable – what then?"[28] he asked. Orwell was well aware that political control did not require the intentional destruction of historical records, just the creation of confusion about the past:

> When there were no external records that you could refer to, even the outline of your own life lost its sharpness. You remembered huge events which had quite probably not happened, you remembered the details of incidents without being able to

recapture their atmosphere, and there were long blank periods to which you could assign nothing.... Even the names of countries, and their shapes on the map, had been different.[29]

The idea that confusion about the past allows control over the present is repeated again and again in the novel. *1984* makes a strong statement about the political consequences of such contemporary phenomena as the neglect of historical studies in schools and universities and the disregard of historical records in political discourse. In his conversation with Winston Smith, O'Brien asks: "Does the past exist concretely, in space? Is there somewhere or other a place, a world of solid objects, where the past is still happening?" When Winston is forced to admit there is not and that the past exists only in the mind, it becomes clear who will have the upper hand. Orwell does not insist that political parties have a better chance to control memory because of the brute force they use but because the holders of memory themselves have given it up. As hinted at by O'Brien, Winston finds himself in a torture chamber not because others have taken control over his mind but for reasons of his own making.

The idea that the destruction of memory is self-imposed is often brought up by critics of post-modernism who claim that the post-modernist fad in universities amounts to sacrifice of the truth by those in charge of its protection. In a keynote address delivered at a meeting of the National Association of Scholars, James Q. Wilson made the following observation:

> In the past, threats to academic freedom or demands for ethnic purity arose from, or were undertaken to placate, forces outside the universities – donors, trustees, parents, and legislators. Today these threats and demands are raised by elements inside the university. In the past such challenges were met by a professioriate that with near unanimity asserted the core principles of the life of the mind: free inquiry based on a commitment to truth and an obligation to conserve as well as advance the culture. Today these threats and demands are met by a professoriate that is deeply divided about the worth of freedom, the possibility of truth, the value of culture, or the meaning of standards.[30]

Using harsher language, Gorman Beauchamp had this to say about the self-inflicted damage to the value of truth:

> Although transmogrified, the smelly little orthodoxies that Orwell despised are still very much with us, and their academic O'Briens are busily at work in their respective Ministries of Love demonstrating to bemused undergraduate Winstons that what they had taken on to be truths are merely cultural constructions not to be counted on.[31]

It is hard to tell how much the notion that no truth exists beyond its reconstruction spread beyond universities' walls into Western cultures. Most of the discourse in this matter is probably just confined to academic circles, but it had two broader political implications.

The first concerns the destructive force of so-called political correctness, i.e., the purification of language in order to avoid offense to suppressed cultures, in the school system. In an important article on "Education after the Culture Wars" published in *Daedalus* in 2002, Diane Ravitch, an historian of education and former assistant secretary of education in the United States, shows how American schools were declining toward "cultural amnesia."[32] She brings many examples showing how "bias and sensitivity review" panels censored information in the name of political correctness, e.g., censoring a fable in which the clever fox persuaded the vain crow to drop her cheese due to apparent gender bias, or a story in which a rotten stump in the forest serves as home to insects, birds, snakes, and other small animals due to its offense to children living in housing projects.

Ravitch surveyed history curricula in American schools that were based on the assumption that historical studies are problematic insofar as they require students to memorize and recall certain facts, abandoning the need to master specific facts and texts for the sake of dubious other skills.

> When we as a nation set out to provide universal access to education, our hope was that intelligence and reason would one day prevail and make a better world, that issues would be resolved by thoughtful deliberation. Intelligence and reason, however, cannot be achieved merely by skill-building and immersion in new

technologies. Intelligence and reason cannot be developed absent the judgment that is formed by prolonged and thoughtful study of history, literature, and culture, not only that of our own nation, but that of other civilizations.[33]

The second implication of the abandonment of the belief in truth concerns people's attitude towards international affairs. In a world in which lies have become an imminent part of the culture – dishonest politicians get elected and nation-states get away with massive deceit – the political order is endangered.

This was a major motive behind the establishment of the Truth and Reconciliation Commission in South Africa. In his opening remarks to the commission's report in 1998, Archbishop Desmond Tutu reminded the world that exploration of the past is invaluable to the construction of a decent political order. The commission, established to explore the crimes committed during the apartheid regime, was criticized for bringing up a past that ought to be forgotten, but Tutu insisted that historical amnesia is more dangerous. Such amnesia will simply not do, he said, because the past refuses to lie down quietly; it has an uncanny habit of returning to haunt one, and one must deal with it for the sake of the future. Tutu realized that lies and deception were at the heart of apartheid – they were indeed its very essence – and therefore led an investigation of the past as a way to establish a different culture of respect for human rights.[34]

Such a concern for historical truth is quite rare in the international arena. Paradoxically, international relations scholars investigating world history were often the first to abandon historical facts for the sake of mechanical models of the international system. During the Cold War, international politics was reduced to systemic models in which a "balance of power" system was replaced by a "tight bi-polar system" which, in turn, transformed into a "loose bi-polar system" and the like. "Equilibrium points," "rules of transformation," and other concepts adopted from general systems theory were used to predict international moves by threatening forces. University graduates often transferred their professors' models to foreign ministries, strategic planning units, and the like. Add to this the general abandonment of historical consciousness as a guide for public life, the anti-historical approach of the mass media, and a post-modernist resentment of historical facts, and one gets a cultural trend of significant political implications.

This trend consists of a view of international politics by scholars, leaders, journalists, and the public at large that ignores the experience gained in hundreds of years of diplomacy, negotiations, mobilizations, wars and peace making, national interests, personal ambitions, craziness, righteous and base motivations, surprise attacks, massacres, human suffering, power shifts, economic depressions, the rise and fall of empires, great leaders, petty thugs, and many other variables that compose international history. With the memory of the historical process lacking, people facing international crises have no way to evaluate them either intelligibly or ethically. Without memory, international politics becomes a game played out by "game theorists," one devoid of the tragic nature of the process, its delicacies and contingencies, and its overall complexity. With historical consciousness playing only a minor role, scholars fail to predict major events (the demise of the Soviet Union was not foreseen by the vast community of analysts) and leaders are willing to subject their populations to risks that had already been proven to be unwarranted in the past.

When history is replaced by a "systems approach" to world affairs, the capacity is lost to make ethical judgments over international affairs. One's ability to distinguish between good and evil depends on historical memory; when no such memory exists, good and evil are determined by the latest image on television. A striking example could be found during the early 1990s when the world stood still for a long time vis-à-vis the massacres taking place in the former Yugoslavia.

In a book titled *The Balkanization of the West*, Stjepan Mestrovic complained about the voyeurism he identified in the Western discourse over the Yugoslavia war. He spoke of the media reports on the war marked by a refusal to take sides. The West, he writes, had put up a good show of moral concern, but all its actions insured that the atrocities in the Balkan continue. He refers to such actions as "The First World Conference of Human Rights" of June 1993 assembled with a broad mandate to discuss human rights as long as it avoids naming any government for abuses, or a feminist convention in Zagreb in October 1992 in which, according to Mestrovic, Western feminists were willing to condemn rape as a male phenomenon but not as a weapon used in the ethnic wars of the Balkans. He is particularly harsh on the media's position that everyone was to blame:

> Despite their feigned objectivity, television anchors and reporters who covered this Balkan war definitely came across as moral agents. They referred to the "warring parties" as representatives of primitive "tribal" and "ethnic" hatreds.

Sixty years earlier, on the eve of World War II, George Orwell was similarly critical of fellow writers, like Henry Miller, who refrained from political commitment and preoccupied themselves with the "self" at a time in which the earth was burning. "To say 'I accept' in an age like our own," he wrote in a critique of Miller's 1935 *Tropic of Cancer*, "is to say that you accept concentration camps, rubber truncheons, Hitler, Stalin, bombs, aeroplanes, tinned food, machine guns, putches, purges, slogans, Bedaux belts, gas masks, submarines, spies, provocateurs, press censorship, secret prisons, aspirins, Hollywood films, and political murders."[35]

Orwell volunteered to fight in the Spanish Civil War of 1936 in which the Spanish republic tried to defend itself unsuccessfully against the rising forces of fascism. It is interesting to note the role of historical memory in his decision to join the republican forces. He went to Spain in late 1936 on behalf of the Independent Labor Party and had little knowledge of the events there but was impressed enough by the cause of the Republic to join the POUM (Partido Obrero de Unificacion Marxista) militia. In *Homage to Catalonia*, where he described his fighting and injury in the war, he admitted:

> In secret I was frightened.... I was old enough to remember the Great War, though not old enough to have fought in it. War, to me, meant roaring projectiles and skipping shards of steel, above all, it meant mud, lice, hunger, and cold.[36]

This is a key sentence not only because Orwell refers in it explicitly to the memory of World War I as an influencing factor but because he demonstrates what that memory consists of. It consists of the reality of war with its actual rather than metaphorical facets – the mud, the lice, etc. War is a horrible experience yet one which constitutes part of the options humanity faced and, in the wake of the fascist threat, a necessary option.

The former imperial policeman knew that there are times in which individuals must get into the trenches and – filled with mud and lice – defend the values they believe in. This sober vision of war, and of the need to engage in war, differed from that of many intellectuals at the time. In his article "Looking Back on the Spanish War" of April 1938, Orwell attacked the leftist intelligentsia in Britain which, he wrote, had swung between the extreme notions of "war is hell" and "war is glorious" both of which are useless:

> At a given moment they may be "pro-war" or "anti-war," but in either case they have no realistic picture of war in their minds.[37]

It is interesting to observe the relationship Orwell proposes between a realistic approach to war and the understanding that war may, at certain historical moments, be inevitable. Although to him war was closer to "hell" than to "glory," this did not justify refraining from it and allowing evil forces to prevail:

> We have become too civilized to grasp the obvious. For the truth is very simple. To survive you often have to fight, and to fight you have to dirty yourself. War is evil, and it is often the lesser evil.[38]

Orwell understood all too well the motivation of those he criticized. These were intellectuals who avoided the complexity of the Spanish situation, which gave them an excuse to remain neutral and leave the stage to the fascists:

> When one thinks of the cruelty, squalor, and futility of war – and in this particular case of the intrigues, the persecutions, the lies and the misunderstandings – there is always the temptation to say: 'one side is as bad as the other. I am neutral.' In practice, however, one cannot be neutral, and there is hardly such a thing as a war in which it makes no difference who wins.[39]

These strong words stem from deep insight into the human condition as it reveals itself in history. Orwell approaches war not in moralistic but in realistic terms, and reality is tragic because human history is tragic. It teaches us that war is bad but that appeasement or a resort to apathy may be worse. In contrast to the warrior's euphoria on one hand, and the pacifist's utopia on the other, Orwell recognizes this state of affairs. To him, only in a world in which two plus two is taken seriously to be four, and cannot be the subject of political or intellectual manipulations, is the distinction between good and evil and the commitment to do good maintained. However, when everything is open to manipulation, when historical facts make no difference, moral commitment is replaced by ethical neutrality. Wars can be fought endlessly without any reason for anybody to care who fights whom, where, when, and why.

To sum up, when Winston Smith puts on paper in large neat capital letters "down with big brother," he expresses resentment against a wide range of phenomena that constitute his world and ours. These include the political communication around him consisting, among other things, of decisions lacking a clear and predictable normative base, misleading rhetoric demanding cognitive and emotional commitments to abstractions he does not share, and a loss of historical memory that turns the world into a blur of signals and images. Winston's desperate attempt to maintain his sanity vis-à-vis big brother by recalling the past and clinging to memory may turn out to be the most significant message of civility stemming from twentieth-century literature.

No Fire; No Smoke; No Rescue

William Golding's *Lord of the Flies* is a complex novel.[1] It is a story of British children who find themselves on an island after a plane crash. This story can be analyzed as a religious allegory of the killing of the messiah; as a didactical tale on the theft of fire; as a fable demonstrating the three Freudian forces: id, ego, and superego; as a moral statement about the imperfection of the human race or, as Virginia Tiger reminds us, simply as an English adventure story. Tiger is right in objecting to an analysis of the novel based on any one of these dimensions.[2] Even a political analysis of *Lord of the Flies* cannot ignore the symbolic and theological dimensions of this tale. And yet, the novel is highly political; it provides important insights into the political world.[3] In particular, *Lord of the Flies* can be read as an espousal of civil society and a call to uphold one of its main features, i.e., reason.

This is a tale about children stranded on an island after a plane crash, children who want to enjoy life and be rescued (with the first wish sometimes prevailing over the second). These are English children who know something about democracy and its rules; they are familiar with the procedures by which leaders are chosen, and when they find out they are alone on the island, they try to establish a functioning community. This is a book about the possibility of actually doing that. Golding can be placed within a glorious tradition in the history of political thought which asks whether individuals who find themselves together on the globe at any given time can live in peace. The question of the chance to survive as a peaceful society stems from the loss of belief in heavenly redemption. It is part of the search for a communal order that would allow the human race to cope collectively with the dangers it faces.

British social contract theorists such as Hobbes and Locke believed in the capacity of humans to form a civilized community. Although they departed from different assumptions about human nature, they believed humans were capable of managing their affairs in a relatively decent manner and able to apply reason in ways that would assure their physical and spiritual survival. Golding, who published *Lord of the Flies* in 1954, may be seen to be updating the question of the social contract, applying it to a world that has experienced World War II. The question is what chance does the human race have to live by a social contract in light of the murderous instinct revealed as so dominant during that war.

The only chance the children on the island have to survive is if they can maintain a fire whose smoke would be seen by a passing ship or plane. In light of the many mystical elements in the novel, the fire may symbolize an aspiration for redemption that would come from the outside, but even from this perspective, redemption depends on the human ability to construct political structures and processes. The chance of survival depends on the ability to maintain a degree of cooperation between members of the community, and Golding expresses great pessimism in this regard.

Golding's idea about the state of the world after World War II is summarized in a sentence toward the end of the novel in which Ralph, the chosen leader, describes the situation: "No fire; no smoke; no rescue."[4] Ralph realizes this when, after a long effort at applying reason, he finds himself isolated in an empty shelter, shivering in the evening sun. This situation can be attributed to the evil nature of the human race but even more so to social conditions. Ralph is not an evil character, nor are many of the other children on the island. Despite some obvious criminal types, such as Roger, we are basically surrounded in this novel with ordinary English schoolchildren, which makes their ability to maintain a fire in order to be rescued all the more interesting and perplexing.

Our first encounter with Ralph is when he jerks up his stockings with an automatic gesture "that made the jungle seem for a moment like the Home Countries."[5] Throughout the book we are reminded that Ralph, like his home country, is part of a long tradition of coping with civility. If there is any hope in the book it depends on him. At the beginning, he stands naked on the sand among the skull-like coconuts looking at the dazzling beach and water. At this point he resembles the biblical Adam who, while still in the Garden of Eden, had a chance.

Ralph has a chance for three reasons. First, because he is not evil by nature; there was mildness about his eyes and mouth, writes Golding, "that proclaimed no devil."[6] Second, because his dad is a commander in the navy and Ralph knows that once he gets leave, he will come to his rescue. Ralph has the confidence gained by many years of British rule over the entire globe: "My father's in the Navy. He said there aren't any unknown islands left. He says the Queen has a big room full of maps and all the islands in the world are drawn there. So the Queen's got a picture of this island,"[7] he reassures the other children. And third, because he uses reason.

Ralph is a natural leader. None of the boys could have found a good reason for his nomination, we are told; there was a stillness about him as he sat that marked him out. But the natural leader shows no signs of arrogance about his mental skills. On the contrary, he is aware of his weaknesses and understands the need to think:

> Listen, everybody. I've got to have time to think things out. I can't decide what to do straight off.[8]

And elsewhere:

> Ralph moved impatiently. The trouble was, if you were a chief you had to think, you had to be wise. And then the occasion slipped by so that you had to grab at a decision. This made you think; because thought was a valuable thing, that got results....[9]

And also:

> There were many things he could do. He could climb a tree; but that was putting all eggs in one basket. If he were detected, they had nothing more difficult to do than wait. If only one had time to think![10]

The essence of wisdom, said Socrates, is modesty, and Ralph is aware of his limitations vis-à-vis the more profound thinker, Piggy:

> Only, decided Ralph as he faced the chief's seat, I can't think. Not like Piggy. Piggy could think. He could go step by step inside that fat head of his, only Piggy was no chief. But Piggy, for all his ludicrous body, had brains. Ralph was a specialist in thought now, and could recognize thought in another.[11]

The skill cherished here is not supreme wisdom but the urge to seek knowledge and the willingness and ability to recognize it. Golding believes in Socratic wisdom, which associates knowledge with the recognition of its limits. It is this association that distinguishes the possessor of reason and turns reason into an effective social force. Ralph's reason has two dimensions. At times it is presented as an almost metaphysical force possessed by few. In chapter 7, when some of the boys search for the beast, Ralph's reason is seen as an inner voice, existing beyond the power of words:

> Now that his physical voice was silent the inner voice of reason, and other voices too, made themselves heard.[12]

Mostly, however, Ralph's reason is presented as a social force combating two alternative forces: the lack of concern with knowledge that characterizes savages like Jack, and the excessive use of intellect embodied in the character of Piggy.

The case of Jack is the more familiar one. When Ralph analyzes the hard conditions on the island, Jack's response is irrational and unreasoned:

> Ralph cleared his throat …

'We're on an island. We've been on the mountain top and seen water all round. We saw no houses, no smoke, no footprints, no boats, no people. We're on an unlimited island with no other people on it.'

Jack broke in.

'All the same you need an army – for hunting. Hunting pigs.'[13]

Jack is a true lunatic with an opaque, mad look reminiscent of fascist leaders in the twentieth century. He is the face of authoritarianism, the antithesis of rational, democratic leadership. Jack's concern with hunting, his shortsightedness and his murderous instincts lead to disaster. Piggy, on the other hand, is far more complex; he seems like a caricature of a twentieth-century intellectual. His language reveals his outsider's status in relation to the group: "Piggy was an outsider, not only by accent, which did not matter, but by fat, and ass-mar, and specs, and a certain disinclination for manual labor."[14] He uses his brain, often in a very creative fashion. He realizes that the plane the boys flew in was shot down in flames, that nobody knows where they are, and that they may stay on the island for a long time. He understands the value of organization and despite his non-charismatic appearance, plays the mandarin's role in taking a count of the boys, asking names and setting rules.

Piggy's disinclination for manual labor does not make him impractical. He comes up with practical solutions, such as the setting of a sundial. His attempts to explain the mathematics of a clock based on the movement of the earth around the sun evoke ridicule but his knowledge is recognized, if only partly:

Piggy was a bore; his fat, his ass-mar and his matter-of-fact ideas were dull, but there was always a little pleasure to be got out of pulling his leg, even if one did it by accident.[15]

At times, the contribution of the helpless boy with the creative brains is invaluable, as when Piggy realizes that the failure to light a fire on the mountain top may not be fatal. He proposes to light a fire on rocks and sand, and it is recognized that "only Piggy could have the intellectual daring to suggest moving the fire from the mountain."[16] However, Piggy's practicality is tied to a tendency to ignore reality when things turn bad.

This is apparent from the beginning when Piggy fails to refrain from revealing his nickname to Ralph, relying on a promise he doesn't get, and has no chance of getting, that it won't be passed on to the others. He is a bore not only because the general population does not know how to relate to his knowledge but because his utilization of it is excessive. His organizational skills resemble those of a clumsy mayor at a town meeting:

> 'That's what I said! I said about our meetings and things and then you said shut up—' His voice lifted into the whine of virtuous recrimination. They stirred and began to shout him down.[17]

Piggy's proposal to regulate the politics of the group with a conch found on the beach is clever, but his reliance on the conch becomes pathetic; he clings to procedures even when they no longer make a difference. Particularly worrisome is Piggy's willingness to escape reality when hard moral consequences must be drawn. Ralph is far less intelligent – he treats the day's decisions as though he were playing chess, writes Golding, but would never be a very good chess player. Yet in contrast to Piggy, he recognizes murder when he faces it and refuses to turn – like Piggy – to escapism. A frightening dialogue takes place after Simon's murder when Piggy sticks to the possibility of calling an assembly and demonstrates a total lack of morality:

> 'Piggy'
> 'uh?'
> 'That was Simon.'
> 'You said that before'
> 'Piggy'
> 'Uh?'
> 'That was murder'
> 'You stop it!' said Piggy, shrilly. 'What good're you doing talking like that?'[18]

This is where Golding's critique of twentieth-century intellectuals is very harsh. It is not sufficient to have brains, but one has to use them in a self-restrained fashion and with moral courage. This is the true mark of reason – common sense that is not devoid of moral judgment and twentieth-century intellectuals have often not shown to possess it. Many of them supported the rise of communist and fascist tyrannies and served in their oppressive bureaucracies,[19] served as their advocates and legitimized them inside their respective countries and abroad.[20] Others presented themselves as resistance fighters while resisting nobody, spending their time instead in writing long manuscripts in coffee houses.[21] Still others refrained from supporting their peers who were persecuted by authoritarian regimes, simply continuing their scholarly or literary activities while the world was burning,[22] and many betrayed the people by holding on to authoritarian dogmas even when freedom was at the horizon.[23]

Mark Lilla describes the adventures of intellectuals such as the pro-Nazi Martin Heidegger and Carl Schmidt, as well as their counterparts in the communist world, under the title *The Reckless Mind*:

> Fascist and Communist regimes were welcomed with open arms by many West European intellectuals throughout the twentieth century, as were countless "national liberation" movements that instantly became traditional tyrannies, bringing misery to unfortunate peoples across the globe. Throughout the century Western liberal democracy was portrayed in diabolical terms as the real home of tyranny – the tyranny of capital, of imperialism, of bourgeois conformity, of "metaphysics," of "power," even of "language." The facts were rarely in dispute; they were apparent to anyone who could read the newspapers and had a sense of moral proportion. No, something deeper was at work in the minds of these European intellectuals, something reckless.[24]

Piggy may be seen as representing those intellectuals who betrayed humanity during the rise of twentieth-century totalitarianism either by excessive reliance on democratic procedures when bolder action had to be taken, or by failing to show courage when it was most needed. Golding is no purist. He does not put his faith in Simon, the saint, whose promise that the boys will be rescued is based on belief, not on reason. Simon's belief is no buffer against the regimented use of brute and wild power by Jack. The world as Golding sees it faces the choice between two options:

> There was the brilliant world of hunting, tactics, fierce exhilaration, skill; and there was the world of longing and baffled common sense.[25]

The community's rescue depends on "the world of longing and baffled common sense" that Ralph walks in – not on Jack's savagery and not on Piggy's intellect. *Lord of the Flies* may thus be read as a novel about the role of reason in the survival of the community. It is not that communal action devoid of reason is no option. Several times in the book the boys engage in activities that strengthen ties and spark the hope that rescue is possible. When a pile of wood is built, for example, the collective effort is described quite enthusiastically:

> [O]nce more, amid the breeze, the shouting, the slanting sunlight on the high mountain, was shed that glamour, that strange invisible light of friendship, adventure, and content.[26]

Golding cherishes collective effort. When the boys light the fire, unkindness melts away and they become "a circle of boys round a camp fire."[27] When they explore the island, they forget in the excitement of exploration the beast they are so frightened by "and soon were climbing and shouting."[28] But collective action itself provides no rescue. Hunting also involves collective action which, however exciting, cannot lead to rescue. In a picture taken from the inventory of fascist images, Ralph and Piggy are attracted to the warmth of the organic tribe. Although it is clear that Jack's tribe had turned into a pile of savages, holding spears, spits, and firewood, developing a circle movement and chanting, the two boys cannot resist the temptation:

> Piggy and Ralph, under the threat of the sky, found themselves eager to take a place in this demented but partly secure society. They were glad to touch the brown backs of the fence that hemmed in the terror and made it governable.[29]

The appeal of the organic tribe is not ignored but neither is the thick, urgent, blind desire to kill that develops as part of it. Thus, the only alternative is the community of reason. Here, this community is compared not only with the organic tribe but also with the democracy of procedure. As shown in the following quotation, the author cannot assure us that such a democracy has a chance to survive when it comes up against stronger forces that do not play by the rules:

> 'Who'll join my tribe and have fun?'
> 'I'm chief,' said Ralph tremulously. 'And what about the fire? And I've got the conch –'
> 'You haven't got it with you,' said Jack, sneering. 'You left it behind. See, clever? And the conch doesn't count on this end of the island –.'[30]

At this point, blowing the conch, calling an assembly and following the right procedures is no longer possible as these procedures are effective only as long as there is general agreement about them. Golding is quite skeptical about the effectiveness of democratic procedures even when there is some agreement:

> 'Meetings. Don't we love meetings? [says Ralph] Every day. Twice a day. We talk.' He got on one elbow. 'I bet if I blew the conch this minute, they'd come running. Then we'd be, you know, very solemn, and someone would say we ought to build a jet, or a submarine, or a TV set. When the meeting was over they'd work for five minutes, then wander off or go hunting.'[31]

The author desires neither the fascist-like organic community nor sheer democratic procedures, but a community that is capable of reasoned collective action. What is missing on the island is mainly civility, which, in this novel, refers to an assemblage of rational, determined individuals who focus on the central tasks of survival. A civilization cannot survive for long only on hunting; the fire must be maintained, which requires a different kind of cooperation than is used in hunting pigs. But such cooperation cannot be found:

> 'Look at us! How many are we? And yet we can't keep the fire going to make smoke. Don't you understand? Can't you see we ought to – ought to die before we let the fire out?'[32]

Part of the reason for the author's focus on children seems to be his understanding that behind the failure of civilization lies the childish fear of beasts and ghosts which hinders rational action and builds up organic tribes of irrational hunters. Here is what Ralph has to say about fear during the search for a beast:

> 'We've got to talk about this fear and decide there's nothing in it. I'm frightened myself, sometimes; only that's nonsense! Like bogies. Then, when we've decided, we can start again and be careful about things like the fire' A picture of three boys walking along the bright beach filtered through his mind. 'And be happy.'[33]

Here lies the novel's message on civility. Individuals are fearful and therefore turn to evil. Making them into saints is infeasible and undesirable. Nor can the state be trusted as a means of bettering them. Jack's choir is a well-organized regiment of disciplined soldiers, but this does not prevent its transformation into savagery. What we are left with is the need to overcome fear and apply reason in our collective action. Reason is not only a precondition of rescue but may actually lead humanity to a degree of happiness – symbolized by those three boys walking, like biblical shepherds, along a bright beach.

Freedom and Responsibility

The twentieth century has witnessed the enormous power of the modern state. Developing since the late Middle Ages, the state has shown its capacity to adopt the great scientific and technological achievements of the human race and harness them to both positive and negative aims. It has been particularly skilled in mobilizing the masses to support these aims and to place itself as the main source of identification. In the mid-twentieth century, one could no longer doubt the power of states to destroy the planet as well as their willingness to utilize that power to commit crimes never before known in history. It was the power of the state that made possible two world wars, the Holocaust, and other acts of genocide, mass enslavement, and the construction of weapons of mass destruction. It was also the power of the state that had to be relied on if humanity was to constrain the destruction and provide for a decent life on the planet.

In the twentieth century, every state was to some degree a "nation-state," namely a state that does not only provide its citizens with protection and well-being but also serves as a focus of their collective aspirations.[1] These aspirations varied from messianic visions to republican considerations, but the fact remains that in all states, individuals were committed in stronger or weaker ways to the acts of the state. Despite great disagreements regarding the degree of commitment that the citizen ought to have, few citizens could escape such a commitment or replace it by a commitment to other human associations. There have always been attempts to weaken the state's grasp over the individual, even acts of refusal to pay taxes or serve in the military forces, but individuals were strongly tied to the state and fulfilled the duties it called for.[2]

There has always been much public discourse about the limits of the state's power and the nature of its relations with the individuals comprising it. Problems of obedience have preoccupied thinkers from early times, but they gained special significance once it became clear, after World War II, how atrocious the actions of states were.[3] Individuals and social groups, in considering their relationship to the state, could not avoid a major question that overshadowed all other questions ever asked in the history of political ideas: the question of responsibility. One need not be a young German in the post-Nazi era, or a communist intellectual after the exposure of Stalin's purges to be concerned with the question of his or her own responsibility for the atrocities committed by the state.

The question of responsibility has been discussed in many forums, the most important of which was the Nuremberg trials after World War II. In these trials of Nazi criminals the question of the individual's duty to obey or refuse an immoral order were thrown into sharp focus. Although the scope was limited to the question of legal responsibility, the trials sparked more general discourse on the responsibility of scientists for the weapons they helped produce,[4] of citizens for wars and acts of genocide committed by their governments,[5] or of rich and strong countries for conditions and events in less advantageous areas.[6]

The ethics of responsibility involved some hard questions: Does an individual's responsibility stem from mere affiliation with the state? Is responsibility shared equally among citizens? What is the relative status of those who command vs. those who obey? Does one's belonging to the bureaucratic, economic, or academic elite increase the responsibility? Is responsibility greater for citizens living in democratic states in which they are presumed to have more control over decisions? What about conscientious objection and civil disobedience – does a citizen's resistance to acts of government reduce his or her responsibility? How active does such resistance have to be? Do persons who frequent anti-government demonstrations bear less responsibility even though these demonstrations turn out to be futile?

Questions related to individual responsibility in view of the atrocities of the twentieth century were forcefully raised by existentialism, originating in the works of Dostoevsky and Kierkegaard, and developed after World War II mainly by Jean Paul Sartre. Existentialism placed the responsibility on the individual's shoulders since existence precedes essence and individual action cannot be blamed on God, history, or nature. As Sartre clarified it in a lecture he gave after the war, individuals are what they make of themselves. Their behavior is not determined by their nature because there is no external force to assure that. "There is no human nature, because there is no God to have a conception of it."[7] Thus, the biblical Abraham, ordered by the voice of an angel to sacrifice his son, is, according to Sartre, responsible for his actions:

> Who ... can prove that I am the proper person to impose, by my own choice, my conception of man upon mankind? I shall never find my proof whatever; there will be no sign to convince me of it. If a voice speaks to me, it is still I myself who must decide whether the voice is or is not that of an angel. If I regard a certain course of action as good, it is only I who choose to say that it is good and not bad. There is nothing to show that I am Abraham.[8]

Sartre clarified that this does not reduce one's responsibility but increases it:

> If ... existence precedes essence and we will to exist at the same time as we fashion our image, that image is valid for all and for the entire epoch in which we find ourselves. Our responsibility is thus much greater than we had supposed, for it concerns mankind as a whole.... Resignation is my will for everyone, and my action is, in consequence, a commitment on behalf of all mankind."[9]

Here then lies a partial answer to the problem of responsibility. Atrocities cannot be attributed to states, leaders, and ideologies but to individuals who are predestined to be free and are therefore responsible before the entire human race for the consequences of their actions. However reluctant we are to recognize our responsibility, especially in light of the complexity of the systems in which we operate, and the scant control we feel we have over them, it is only our own will and conscience that will be judged in the last resort. The state may have failed the moral test, but this does not reduce the responsibility of the individuals comprising it.

Camus's *The Stranger* makes this point in full vigor through its main protagonist. Camus was born in 1913 in the village of Mondovi to a father of Alsatian origin and a Spanish mother. His father died a year later in the battle of the Marne, and the child grew up in extremely poor conditions in the working-class district of Belcourt. Since he was an excellent student, with the help of an enlightened uncle, he made it to the university of Algiers and later to France, where he became one of the important philosophers, writers, and playwrights of the age. During the war he lived mostly in Oran and completed his major works: the novels *The Stranger* and *The Plague*, the play *Caligula*, and the philosophical treatise *The Myth of Sisyphus*. He joined the resistance and wrote for the underground paper *Combat*. Camus met Sartre in 1943 and became very close to him until their break in the early 1950s over Sartre's boundless support of Russian communism at the time. In 1957 Camus won the Nobel Prize and in 1960 was killed in a car accident. His autobiographical novel *The First Man* was published posthumously.

The Stranger begins with the famous words: "Mother died today. Or maybe yesterday, I don't know."[10] It is easy to consider this phrase one of defiance and revolt, especially in light of the emphasis placed by the court judging Meursault, and by Camus in his later interpretations of the book, on Meursault's failure to cry at his mother's funeral. But it can also be read as a statement about one's helplessness in the face of a mother's death. One could react differently to a dry telegram announcing the death of a mother than Meursault does, by remarking, "That doesn't mean anything. It may have been yesterday."[11] But the fact of the matter is that it really does not mean anything as far as one's capacity to do anything about it is concerned, and it could indeed have been yesterday. It is understandable why Meursault's insistence that his mother's death was not his fault was taken to represent the rejection of common conventions, but as it was not his fault, he may be seen to be commenting on the constraints in which he lives.

Occasionally Meursault behaves in an unconventional way in defiance of the chains that shackle him. Thus, instead of mourning his mother in the conventional way, he goes to a Fernandel movie and makes love to Marie Cordona. But such independent responses to his mother's death do not diminish the fatalism implied by that death nor do they diminish the helplessness involved. The sense of fatalism, developed later in *The Myth of Sisyphus*, appears faintly in *The Stranger*, as if the young Camus still refused at this stage to submit to it. But however defiant Meursault's behavior is, there is no way out of the determining factors. This is usually hinted at in relation to trivial matters as when Meursault is reminded during the funeral by a nurse that "if you go slowly, you risk getting sun-stroke. But if you go too fast, you perspire and then in the church you catch a chill."[12] "She was right. There was no way out,"[13] he responds.

Determinism is apparent in the mythological relationship between old Salamano and his dog. Although the man and the dog hate each other, they are connected to each other by a strong bond. After living together for so long, the retired railway worker and the spaniel with skin disease walk alike and look alike, as if they belonged to the same species. The scene in which they drag each other along may be read as a statement about common fate:

> You can see them in the rue de Lyon, the dog dragging the man along until old Salamano stumbles. Then he beats the dog and swears at it. The dog cringes in fear and trails behind. At that point it's the old man's turn to drag it along.[14]

When asked what the dog has done, the old man's answer reveals the deterministic nature of the relationship: "He's always there."[15] When the dog gets lost, his owner may not be willing to pay money to get him back, but he is lost himself, as there is no way for him to escape the symbiosis. It may be easier for Camus to admit the lack of control we have over our affairs when it comes to the old man than to his main character. Salamano, we learn, wanted to go into the theatre but ended up as a railway worker and did not regret it because this provided him with a small pension. We may thus assume that Meursault too, despite his independence of will, has been dragged along by circumstances. Even his shooting of an Arab – one of the most notorious acts of free will in modern literature – can be attributed to circumstances ranging from Marie waking him up that Sunday morning to the political situation in Algeria.

In his analysis of *The Stranger*, Connor Cruise O'Brien suggests that in order to comprehend the book one must understand the relationship between Camus, who grew up among the poorest of the European working class, and the Moslem and Arabic-speaking people who made up the bulk of the population in Algeria. In light of the little information Camus provides us with about that relationship, O'Brien characterizes him as a writer who attempts to escape his origins and to belong instead to the intellectual culture of the French middle class. According to O'Brien, Camus reveals himself as incapable of thinking in any other categories than those of a Frenchman; his Mediterranean culture is a European one and in Algeria a French one. This, says O'Brien, explains his and his protagonist's estrangement. Like a Crusader, Camus is a stranger both on the African shore and in France. By positioning Camus in this way O'Brien is able to advance the argument that the book presents a myth of French Algeria in which no French court would actually have condemned a European to death for shooting an Arab. What appears to the casual reader a contemptuous attack on the court, writes O'Brien, is not in fact an attack at all but a denial of colonial reality.[16]

However, colonial reality is by no means denied, and Camus actually reveals to us a great deal about the Algerian situation. I would like to argue that *The Stranger* exposes some of the deepest truths about the life of two peoples doomed to live with each other on the same piece of land. Like Salamano and his dog, they hate each other but find themselves in a bond that cannot be untied in spite of the suffering it involves.

The Algerian scene must be recognized. Commentators have pointed at various elements of "pied-noir" culture in the novel, e.g., the excursion on the beach in which such elements as the values of the body, the lack of reflection, the camaraderie, and the superficial sense of belonging to nature have been identified.[17] But it is not only the French perspective we are exposed to. Although Algeria does not appear in this novel in the colorful way in which it is depicted in *The First Man*, it is there, with the people, the clothing, the crowded trams, the cafés, the Sunday football fans, and, of course, the eternal cinemas.

Camus provides a beautiful picture of a North African town on "A typical Sunday."[18] He describes families out for a walk with the boys in sailor suits, with trousers below their knees, looking a bit cramped in their stiff clothing, and a little girl with a big pink bow and black patent leather shoes, an enormous woman in a brown silk dress and a small, frail father wearing a straw hat, a bow tie and carrying a walking stick. The local lads are described with their hair greased back, red ties, tight-fitting jackets with embroidered handkerchiefs in their top pockets and square-toed shoes. The trams are described as they return from the local football ground with bunches of spectators perched on the steps and hanging from the guardrails. We are also exposed to the moment, so familiar in that setting, when the local cinemas pour their audiences out in a great flood onto the street.

Against this background, Camus describes the Algerian situation as only an insider, not an estranged outsider, could do. Algeria was annexed to France in 1836. By the time Camus wrote the novel, the French minority and the Arab majority had been living side by side for many generations in a state of mutual dependency that involved a great deal of fear. That condition was forcefully described in *The First Man*:

> [T]his was the very country into which he felt he had been tossed, as if he were the first inhabitant, or the first conqueror, landing where the law of the jungle still prevailed, where justice was intended to punish without mercy what custom had failed to prevent – around him these people, alluring yet disturbing, near and separate, you were around them all day long, and sometimes friendship was born, or camaraderie, and at evening they still withdrew to their closed houses, where you never entered, barricaded also with their women you never saw, or if you saw them on the street you did not know who they were, with faces half veiled and their beautiful eyes sensual and soft above the white cloth, and they were so numerous in the neighborhoods where they were concentrated, so many of them that by their sheer numbers, even though exhausted and submissive, they caused an invisible menace that you could feel in the air....[19]

Now, consider the central scene of the novel. Meursault's killing of an Arab on the beach has been seen as a deliberate act of murder committed in isolation from any moral essence, although not from the need to pay a price

Freedom and Responsibility / 105

for it. What could be less moral than the shooting of a man by a person declaring: "I realized at that point that you could either shoot or not shoot."[20] This is the same person who, a few pages before, told us the following: "That evening, Marie came round for me and asked me if I wanted to marry her. I said I didn't mind and we could do so if she wanted to."[21]

Yet, it is hard not to recognize the determinism involved in the scene. It takes place under the burning sun. "[T]he bright morning sunshine hit me like a slap in the face."[22] "The sun was shining almost vertically onto the sand and the glare from the sea was unbearable."[23] The bright sun stands in contrast to the shady streets of the Algerian town in the evenings described in *The First Man*. In those evenings there was tension and fear but also a state of ambivalence that allowed French settlers and Arab inhabitants to coexist for generations. But in the bright sun there is no escape. In the murder scene Meursault seeks escape to no avail:

> And every time I felt the blast of its hot breath on my face, I set my teeth, closed my fists in my trouser pockets and tensed my whole body in defiance of the sun and of the drunken haze it was pouring into me.[24]

He hopes to relax in the shade, but there is no shade, just the bare reality, lit up by a burning sun, of two peoples on the same land. Thus, you could either shoot or not shoot, but it is clear the shots will come. What I am arguing is that the shooting on the beach is the deterministic outgrowth of an impossible political situation. We may not predict when the shots will come, or who will do the shooting, but the murder is unavoidable.

In trying to make sense of the murder, or to comprehend its senseless nature, it is easy to ignore the deterministic elements in chapter 6 in which the scene is described. Camus himself had hidden those elements, possibly even from himself, by placing Meursault on trial where the act is related to human choice rather than to political reality. But I would like to present a different perspective admittedly stemming from my own background as an Israeli. This perspective developed in my thought mainly after the assassinations of President Anwar Sadat of Egypt in 1981 and Prime Minister Yitzhak Rabin of Israel in 1995. These murders, like the one in *The Stranger*, represent neither sheer individual choices nor mythological sacrifices, although they were often interpreted as such, but rather acts stemming from given political circumstances. It is unknown who will pull the trigger – in the specific situation on the beach Meursault was not the one who would come first to mind – but the murder would ultimately occur, for in the above circumstances, there is no choice.

Only a writer living in a country claimed by two peoples can describe the scene in the way Camus did. The murder has no real reason besides fear. The fear is not just of the Arabs as "the others" but of their being so deeply rooted in the locale. This is apparent in every word relating to the Arabs in the scene:

> We were just about to set off when Raymond suddenly pointed across the street. I looked and saw a group of Arabs leaning against the front of the tobacconist's shop. They were looking at us in silence, but in their own special way, as if we were nothing more than blocks of stone or dead trees.[25]

This is the look of the native who has been there before, will be there later, and assumes that the presence of the French settler is temporary. Throughout the scene the Arab patience is stressed, mainly in a description of two Arabs lying down behind a large rock "quite calm and almost contented. Our arrival had no effect on them,"[26] one of them watching the intruders in silence, the other blowing a small reed, the symbol of pastoral native life since ancient times.

The deterministic element is strengthened by the fact that the French in the scene, like many Europeans in colonial history, are constantly on the move while the Arabs are mostly situated in motionless silence. There is a jumpiness about the Europeans who are on the beach for fun. But this cannot hide the fact that, beyond the picturesque rows of little villas with green or white fences along which they walk and the motionless surface of the sea, there is commotion that can be expected to burst forth at any moment. Particularly strong is the scene in which the small group of Pied Noirs is walking towards a bus stop:

> We went towards the bus stop which was a bit further along and Raymond informed me that the Arabs weren't following us. I

looked round. They were still in the same place and looking with the same indifference at the spot where we'd just been.[27]

Such images of fear and insecurity make it clear that the specifics of the coming struggle are not very important. Indeed, the shooting has no real reason, but it is also unavoidable as Meursault realizes: "Whether I stayed there or moved, it would come to the same thing."[28]

Returning now to the issue of responsibility, does such lack of control over the circumstances imply that nobody is really responsible for the shooting on the beach? Here lies Camus' contribution to political thought; he separates the question of responsibility we have over the circumstances surrounding us from the degree of control we have to change them. In other words, he breaks the tie between freedom and responsibility. We have no control over the circumstances and at the same time we have full responsibility. This is why Meursault accepts his trial and verdict with such apparent indifference. It is not defiance of the legal or political system. It is the acceptance, and internalization, of his condition. None of us has control over the political circumstances, but this does not remove the responsibility we have, as citizens, over the acts committed in our name by the modern state.

And History Continues

Elsa Morante's *History* may be read as a political novel in every sense of the term. It tells the history of the twentieth century and while doing so suggests invaluable insights on the politics of that century. This is not an obvious point for we usually tell political history differently. We write it from the perspective of the political leaders and events that shaped it. The telling of history has always accompanied its makers, whether explicitly – when historians have served as writers of annals and myths – or implicitly – when they did so unconsciously as "fellow travelers." Even when historians left the courts of the kings and rulers who were their patrons, and had to earn their living by selling their trade to the general public, they never abandoned the tendency, developed over many years of patron–client relations, to place political leaders at the center stage of political history.

Therefore, in a book telling the history of the twentieth century we usually expect to find such hooligans as Hitler, Stalin, and Mussolini starring in the narrative. Historians are forever preoccupied with the lives of these figures, the social, economic, and political conditions that brought them to power, the political regimes they constructed, the states and lives they destroyed, and the international moves they initiated.

Elsa Morante writes not the history of the hooligans but of hooliganism. This may have something to do with her own life. She was born in Rome in 1918 as the daughter of a Sicilian father and Emilian mother. Her formal education was incomplete, and she left home at the age of eighteen. She became involved in Italy's literary circles where she met and married the writer Alberto Moravia. During World War II they lived the life of refugees in the countryside near Cassino. Her first novel, *House of Liars*, was published in 1948, her next novel, *Arturo's Island*, nearly a decade later, and *History* in 1974. She died in Rome in November 1985.

History is the political history of the mid-twentieth century written from the unique perspective of a woman who, unlike many historians, is not fascinated by the leaders who shaped the events. From the point of view of the protagonist Ida Ramundo, it really does not matter whether the leader presently dominating the scene is called Hitler, Stalin, or Mussolini. Ida is a woman who tries to survive, and as we are studying political history by focusing on her private sphere, it takes a different turn. Ida's age, we learn, was thirty-seven, and she certainly made no effort to seem younger. Her rather undernourished body, the withered bosom, the lower part awkwardly fattened, was more or less covered by an old woman's brown overcoat, with a worn fur collar and a grayish lining whose tattered edges could be seen hanging from the cuffs of the sleeves. She was a teacher born to a Jewish mother who, due to an animal-like foresight, had her baptized. She is the mother of Nino, born in 1925 to a father who died of "the disease of our time"[1] – cancer, and of Useppe born in 1941 as a result of Ida's rape by a Nazi soldier.

In one of the first pages of the book we learn of Ida's nightmare dreams complementing her daytime life "with pauses and recurrences, to the end, entwining around her days more like a parasite or prison-guard than a companion."[2] In one of these dreams, she saw herself running in a place gloomy with soot or with smoke (factory, or city, or slum), clutching to her bosom a little doll, naked and a vermilion color, as if it had been dipped in red paint. This image may be seen as the motto of the entire novel. *History* is the history of the years 1941 to 1947, the most horrifying and disgusting years in the history of humankind, from the perspective of an undernourished woman holding her baby, who will die at the age of six, and trying to survive with him. When seen from this perspective, the historical events differ from their presentation in common historical narratives in three ways: they lose their uniqueness, their glory fades, and any hope that could be pinned on them is lost. For the image of the mother holding a baby in her arms, hopelessly trying to survive, is repeated again and again in history.

History thus provides us with major insights on twentieth-century history. It tells that history in total detachment from notions stressing its messianic nature. It reminds us that we live in history, not in an a-historical era in which people and events are seen in a unique, glorious, and hopeful light. All the grand ideologies coming to power in the twentieth century – communism, fascism, and no less so industrial capitalism, the ideology cherishing the modern industrial state – attributed a grand design to history. They endowed leaders with vision, pictured events as exceeding their time and place, and added a purpose – mostly a utopian one – to the historical process. Individuals were seen as components in the grand design, and events were explained accordingly. The state was no longer the seventeenth- and eighteenth-century construct intended to provide its citizens with security but a sacred entity. In this novel, however, nothing of that sacredness remains. At the beginning of each chapter, the historical events of the era are presented in the dry, schematic language in which they appear in history textbooks. Yet, to the readers of this novel, influenced by the above perspective, the events seem very different:

"The latest scientific discoveries concerning the structure of matter mark the beginning of the atomic century,"[3] writes Morante in the dry language in which Ida, the schoolteacher, probably taught these events in the classroom. But she does not allow us to gloat over the discoveries of the scientific age, which fascinated the twentieth century, as we are also aware that nothing new will happen in the world as a result. Like all centuries and millennia that have preceded it, to Elsa Morante and her character "the twentieth century also observes the well-known, immobile principle of historical dynamics: power to some, servitude to others."[4] When history is taught by focusing on the holders of power – the kings, the noblemen, and the dictators – it may appear to be rather glorious. Even the history of the great clash between the bourgeoisie and the proletariat may seem festive. But to Ida it does not matter much what force will win in any battle of history, not even in the battle of the proletariat she belongs to, because even when the proletariat wins, she will find herself with her child in search of rescue.

Therefore, all the historical writings declaring the victory of one power over another in this book turn into nonsense. We are reminded of the moments of glory in the century which lose their glory simply because they are presented not from the perspective of the victors, or their fellow travelers, but from that of a woman who is conscious of the fact that the gap between those destined to power and those to servitude never closes. In this book, the founding of the Comintern in Moscow in 1919 with the pretension of summoning all of the world's proletariat, regardless of race, language, or nationality, to the common goal of revolutionary unity, amid the massacres, epidemics, and poverty of the civil war simply seems crazy. Mao Tse-tung's long march in which he led 130,000 men of his Red Army across 7,500 miles of Chinese land to elude the preponderant forces of the nationalist government becomes less glorious than it is depicted in most history books once we identify not only with the 30,000 who survived the march, but also with the 100,000 who did not.

The world leaders seem so different in this book than they do in the tales and pictures inspired by their great deeds. To Ida, Benito Mussolini is nothing other than a mediocre opportunist, a combination of all the worst flotsam of Italy. His invasion of Abyssinia, which promoted Italy from a kingdom to an empire, leaves little impression on her; it seems as remote an event as the Punic wars. In the Italian classroom where she taught, at the center of the wall, just above her desk, next to the Crucifix, there were enlarged framed photographs of the new King-Emperor. In the tradition of King-Emperors, Mussolini is portrayed on the wall as a heroic figure, but Ida remains unimpressed, for "in reality, with the exaggerated jut of the chin, the artificially clenched jaws, and the mechanical dilation of eye-sockets and pupils, it resembled more a vaudeville clown playing a sergeant scaring recruits."[5] As we shall see later, the horrors of Nazism are treated in this book very seriously, but this does not make Hitler less of a failure and serf, sick with a vindictive sense of inferiority.

Even the victory over the forces of evil is not drawn in other colors than those by which the victims of history view it. The end of World War I is presented here in the form of seventy people seated at the peace table, to re-divide the world among them and to draw the new map of Europe. After dragging us for hundreds of pages through the horrors of World War II, Elsa Morante, in contrast, say, to Time-Life photos or Hollywood films, gives us no respite even when victory over Nazism has been finally reached. We are not allowed to treat it in apocalyptic terms because, despite the various "summit meetings" in which the great personalities of the age are busy re-establishing some kind of appropriate order, not much can change for Ida:

> The landowners still held the land, the industrialists the machinery and the factories, the officers their ranks, the bishops their dioceses. And the rich were fed at the expense of the poor, who then aimed, in their turn, at taking the place of the rich, according to the general rule.[6]

This novel provides us with a rare opportunity to learn about the events neither from the perspective of the rich nor of the poor. Ida, says the author, belonged to a third species that lives and dies and gives no news of itself, except at times, perhaps, in the crime reports. One of the powerful scenes in the book concerns Ida's mother, Nora, whose death did not even make the crime reports. In the summer of 1938, amidst official anti-Semitic propaganda, word is spread of an imminent census of all the Jews of Italy. All imaginable forms of near and future persecutions become confused in her mind, and she decides to emigrate. The story of Jewish emigration to Palestine in the 1930s has often been told in heroic terms inspired by the rhetoric of the Jewish national movement – Zionism – but never had it been told from the perspective of a sixty-eight-year-old Jewish woman of the "third species" who goes to the coast in search of some freighter flying an Asian flag, where she finds, of course, her death. Needless to say, this story, stripped of any heroism, is the more realistic and common one for Jews in 1938.

This special perspective generates very different insights on major political movements and ideas in the twentieth century, especially on anarchism, fascism, and Nazism.

Even after the demise of the grand ideologies of the modern era, and the sober realization that their messianic rhetoric had mostly been a deception, many still maintain a warm place in their hearts for anarchism. Possibly because anarchism has never come to power as communism and fascism did, it remained in its purity – an ideology of the young and restless who are truly seeking a better world. Anarchism is a belief in the replacement of government authority by a political order based on cooperation. Inspired by thinkers like Gandhi and Tolstoy, anarchism became largely associated with pacifism, and its origins were traced to early Christian communities. Even when anarchists were advocating the use of violence, they were treated with a touch of romanticism stemming from the movement's naïveté, secrecy, and international reach.

The book is filled with anarchists, but from its special perspective, anarchism loses its romantic flavor. Here, it is associated with Ida's father Giuseppe, teacher and drunk, who shouts anarchist slogans on Sunday in his house. He feels a sense of betrayal because, as an employee of the state, he betrays his comrades and brothers. As a teacher, he would have to preach anarchy in school, but this can be done only in romantic visions of anarchism while Ida's father has a family to feed. Thus he settles for his own house where he shouts the slogans accompanied by exact references ("Freedoms are not granted, they are seized. Kropotkin!") while his worried wife, Nora, would run to close the doors and windows, to muffle these subversive notions from the ears of neighbors or passersby. Anarchism is thus stripped of its romanticism and turns into a set of slogans shouted by a drunk "like a wagon-driver singing to the moon."[7] In a sense, Elsa Morante returns anarchism to what it really was in modern history – a marginal ideology. The only place where Giuseppe can share his views is a tavern in which he meets with other "poor Sunday anarchists."[8] Even there, a traitor can be found.

A more serious encounter with anarchism is given us through the figure of Vivaldi Carlo who tries to reconcile between anarchism and pacifism in a world in which such reconciliation is hopeless. Here is a conversation between Carlo and Ida's son Nino:

> 'My-ideals-REJECT-violence. All evil is derived from violence!'
> 'Then what kind of anarchist does that make you?'
> 'True anarchism cannot admit violence. The anarchist ideal is the negation of power. And power and violence are the same thing...'

'But without violence how can you manage to have an Anarchist Government?'

'Anarchism rejects Government ... And if the means has to be violence, then it's no good. We don't pay the price. In this case, Anarchism isn't achieved.'

'Then, if it isn't going to get done, I don't like it. I like things that get done.'

No wonder Carlo's anarchism ends up where Giuseppe's did, as part of a drunk's sermon in a tavern on Sunday. In a very moving scene towards the end of the book, Carlo, who is by now known by his real name Davide, expresses his views about anarchism. The author is sympathetic to the cause yet also aware that it has no chance. This is conveyed to us in the form of a long, confused speech made to card-players in the tavern who show no interest whatsoever. The description of the scene seems like a confession by the author about her helplessness vis-à-vis her own writing. She writes a huge book on the horrors of the twentieth century, knowing she has no chance to prevent future horrors: "And when I try to recapitulate his talk that afternoon in the tavern," says the author about Davide's sermon, "I see it in the image of many horses chasing one another around a circular track, always passing the same spots."[9]

Indeed, Davide, haunted in 1947 by the burden of the evils exposed in World War II, does not find the means to communicate them in a way that would spark interest or commitment. As the anarchist sermon goes on over many pages, its academic nature becomes clear. In the real world, what existed in the past will be in the future, as the following dialogue illustrates:

Suddenly, Davide took umbrage, and breaking off his speech, he pulled the chair up behind him, silenced. But before flinging himself down on it again, with sudden resolve, he thrust out his chest towards the company seated around him. And in a self-accusatory tone (though with a provocative brutality, which was the equivalent of a fist brought down hard on the table), he cried:

'I was a bourgeois!'

'And I' replied the old man with the medal, not looking at him but with a frank and kindly laugh, 'was born a porter at the wholesale Market'[10]

Fascism is presented as no less ridiculous than anarchism. Through the story of Nino, Ida's elder son, we learn about the rise, upbringing, and behavior of a fascist. Again, from the special perspective of this book, we are exposed to a unique image of fascism; Nino is first and foremost a "little street ruffian."[11] Our first encounter with him is through a photograph portraying him as:

> [A] little hoodlum of perhaps fifteen or sixteen, wrapped in a sumptuous camel's-hair coat, which he wore as if it were a flag. Between the fingers of his right hand you could vaguely discern a cigarette's whiteness; and his left foot rested on the running-board of a custom-built sports car (parked there at random by some unknown owner), with the masterful attitude of tiger-hunters, in the great forests.[12]

This photograph points at fascism, at least in its Italian version, as nothing more than a tendency by a half-baked hooligan to resemble the images spread by popular culture. He may feel masterful, but there is little he truly masters – his foot is on a car that does not belong to him and may disappear soon from under it. The effect of popular culture stands out in the description of his room, which does not differ much from that of every other teenager:

> On the wall, over the bed, in the place of holy pictures, there were various photographs, cut out of magazines and held by thumbtacks, of movie actresses in bathing suits or evening dress: the most spectacular had been marked with great scrolls in red pencil, so emphatic they seemed the trumpet signals of an assault, or the cries of an amorous cat out hunting. On the same wall, but to one side, and also attached with thumbtacks, there was also a copy of a poster showing a Roman eagle clutching the British Isles in its talons.[13]

This does not reduce the danger of fascism but demonstrates its adolescent nature. It is merely a meaningless set of slogans used by a fifteen-year-old. This becomes very clear in a scene in which Nino asks his mother for pocket money to party. In the somewhat routine conversation between the son and his mother, he boasts he will end up chief of the Black Brigades and fight for the fatherland and for the Duce, but it is hard to take him seriously:

> The excess of defiance in his voice as he uttered these capitals, betrayed a blasphemous intention. You could sense that, in his boyish demands, Fatherlands and Duces, and the whole theater of the world, were reduced to a farce, which had value only because it agreed with his rage to live.[14]

Fascism then is reduced to a farce fitting a teenager's rage. Therefore, when it will no longer fit him, other ideals and leaders will be sought. Nino will join the partisans in the forests, admire Stalin, and when Stalin will disappoint him, aim at the next scene fitting his rage to live – American capitalism. Elsa Morante tells us that all ideologies, movements, and leaders are only anchors for the Ninos of the world. Here is Nino speaking about himself:

> Stalin and the other Big Cheeses, it's all one system: they play footies with each other to screw everybody else and to screw each other, too. And Nino doesn't give a shit about them. Nino wants to live, he wants to enjoy all life and all the world, all the universe! With the suns, moons, and planets!!! Now, 1946, it's America's big moment ... Nino ... wants to get rich, a superbillionaire, and go off to America in a special de luxe plane.[15]

Nazism however is very different. The terror of Nazism is presented in its full horror in a rape scene. The depiction of the Nazi soldier raping Ida as a confused adolescent magnifies the horror a thousand times. When we encounter Gunther at the opening of the novel, he seems like a caricature of a boy turned soldier:

[I]n contrast with his martial stride, he had a separate expression in his eyes. His face betrayed an incredible immaturity, although he was six feet tall, more or less.[16]

Dressed in a uniform short at the waist and in the sleeves, Gunter lives in Dachau in which 66,428 corpses will be found during the liberation in 1945. When Ida meets him on a January day of 1941, however, Dachau is still a rural village and Gunter is a young German soldier shipped to Italy while thinking he was being sent to Africa. He suffers from loneliness and melancholy and broods constantly in bitter compassion about a prostitute in Munich, who had lost a customer.

When Ida, that "decent-looking thing, coming home just at that moment, laden with shopping bags and purse"[17] encounters the Nazi soldier before her house, she stares at him with an absolutely inhuman gaze, as if confronted by the true and recognizable face of horror. And she is right. The humble soldier described as "a mamma's boy"[18] is indeed an embodiment of absolute horror. The fears haunting the Jewish woman, writes the author, prevented her from seeing anything of him except a German army uniform. And on meeting, at the very door of her home, that uniform which seemed to be stationed there, waiting for her, she thought she had arrived at the terrible rendezvous preordained for her since the beginning of the world. But this is exactly the point. When the Nazi atrocities became known, the world had difficulty in attributing them to regular German boys, but Ida's perspective places the atrocities where they belong – as the deeds of eighteen-year-old mamma's boys.

In 1941, the Nazis are those in power, and thus, from Ida's perspective, there is no escape, just as there is no exit from the room in which she finds herself with her rapist. As a victim of history, she is aware that even when Gunter falls asleep in her bed, and it seems easy to kill him, this cannot be done. For the killing of rapists who fall asleep is done in biblical myths, but very rarely in real life:

> It would have been easy, now, to kill him, following the example of Judith in the bible, but Ida, by nature, couldn't conceive such an idea, not even as a fantasy.[19]

The scene turns both more realistic and surrealistic when Gunter wakes up and rushes to fix a loose wire that causes a light in the room to flicker. Elsa Morante places the traditional eagerness of many men to fix light sockets and of many women to be afraid to do the job themselves, in a rape scene between a Nazi soldier and a Jewish woman. The woman "observed him in mute admiration, because in her (as in certain primitive peoples) there remained a timid, unconfessed distrust of electricity and its phenomena."[20]

Through such literary means, the horrors of the Nazis are attributed to the real people who committed them. When Adolph Eichmann, for example, was brought to justice in Jerusalem and the world watched his trial, it was extremely difficult to adjust to the fact that he looked not like a monster but like a regular clerk. This dissonance caused Hanna Arendt to develop her theory about the banality of evil, according to which evil is embodied in regular people.[21] Gunter is a strong literary expression of that theory. Elsa Morante makes us realize that the historical encounter between ultimate brutality and its victims can be found on a January morning in an Italian home where a soldier whose last name is not even known, and who will die within three days in an air attack, fixes a light socket.

I would like to argue that the special perspective we get on twentieth-century history by learning about it through the eyes of Ida Ramundo makes a significant contribution to modern political theory. It casts doubt on the utopian – messianic connotations that have been added to that theory since the French revolution. Let me explain this point. Despite the expectations that the scientific revolution would enhance pragmatic and realistic attitudes in the world, utopian yearnings have remained an essential component of twentieth-century political thought. Utopianism is the postulation of a definite goal or preordained finale to history, for the attainment of which you need to recast all aspects of life and society in accordance with some very explicit principle.

Utopian notions have deep origins in Christian millennial theology.[22] We find them in the Book of Revelations' promise of Christ's second coming and his rule for a thousand years on earth, followed by a second judgment and resurrection, after which the righteous will live in peace with God. We also find them in political theory from St. Augustine's "city of God," through Rousseau's general will to Marx's rule of the proletariat. The notion that a utopian political order may be prepared for on earth has been labeled by Jacob Talmon "political messianism."[23]

Political messianism can be found in the national movements of Europe as well as in those of Asia and Africa where utopian promises made against a religious background functioned as a source of mass mobilization. National leaders often used messianic rhetoric in which the construction of the modern state was associated – metaphorically or not – with the coming of the messiah. The state was not conceived just as a political association but as a framework for the fulfillment of utopian desires. Whether the utopia was Platonic, Augustinian, or socialist, it was part of the political discourse even in societies in which the messiah was seen merely as a metaphor.

The discourse over political messianism has focused mainly on its cost. The question was not whether rule by Plato's philosopher king, Augustine's God, or Marx's proletariat is desirable in its pure form, but whether it can be implemented on earth without enormous cost. Karl Popper's *The Open Society and its Enemies* threw light on the cost of any heavenly utopia whose implementation on earth requires the suppression of traditional political forms. Utopians – notably Marx – have realized the cost but believed that it is worth paying it in return for a just, universal order and a redeeming society. This was in line with religious messianic movements that have realized since the biblical prophet Ezekiel that a terrible war would precede the messianic age of peace on earth.

History adds an important phase to the discourse on political messianism. It takes a wholly different orientation in regard to the coming of the real or metaphorical messiah. It does not deal with the desirability, feasibility, or cost of redemption. It does not involve itself in the theological questions about the coming of the Messiah in the religious or political sense. In this book, the chance of the human race to reach utopia and redeem itself is not a question whose answer depends on events in the end of days, or on acts to be committed in order to hasten the coming of the Messiah. *History* makes an original point: the Messiah has already been here, on earth. He lived among us in the years 1941 to 1947, the dreadful years of human history, but his coming has made no difference whatsoever. Thus, the book brings us back from millennial dreams to history as we know it. It kills our hopes for redemption of any kind by claiming not that the messiah cannot come, would not come, or should not come because of the cost involved, but that he has already been here and still we have not been redeemed.

History provides no hope for redemption from the historical process with its bureaucratic institutions, social structures, and moral evils. This idea is conveyed through the character of Useppe, Ida's younger son born as a result of the rape, who may be seen as symbolizing the messiah. His birth is reminiscent of the birth of another messiah in Bethlehem:

> The infant was so small he could fit comfortably in the midwife's two hands, as in a basket. And after having proved himself by the heroic enterprise of coming into the world on his own, he hadn't even the voice to cry. He announced his presence with a whimper so faint he seemed a little lamb, born last and forgotten in the straw.[24]

Useppe comes into the world with his own strength, in order not to cost suffering to others. He is pure, innocent, sinless, virtuous, sick and will die at the age of six. He accompanies his mother in the horrible events of the midcentury but is never affected by them. He is always there, side by side with the actors, touching-not-touching them, like a floating angel. A typical image is that of the naked child sleeping between two armed warriors in a war shelter for refugees. Another image is that of his brother Nino going to fight for the Duce in a battalion of Blackshirts, solemnly shaking Useppe's little hand, "in a real pact of honor and importance."[25] From the beginning, when Ida is terrified about Nino finding her illegal half-Jewish child in the house, there is brotherly love there; Nino even brings friends home to see the smiling baby and nothing bad happens. While Nino gives political sermons in the house, which lead his appalled mother to take refuge in her room, the child, "would stay in a corner to gaze at his brother with great respect, but with no fear: as if he were facing a volcano too high to strike him with its lava. Or as if he were in the midst of a stupendous storm at sea, through which he was recklessly passing his tiny boat."[26]

A particularly strong image of the child as "touching-not-touching" history is presented in the story of the newspaper. One day a vendor in a kiosk made a hat from a newspaper, like a carabiniere's headgear, to amuse Useppe. Shortly afterwards, on a Sunday in June 1945, Useppe found a sheet of paper in which some fruits were wrapped, thinking, perhaps, of making himself a carabiniere's hat. The magazine included photographs and the relentless author informs us what they depicted:

> 1) a heap of murdered prisoners, naked and sprawling, and already partly decomposed; 2) a huge quantity of piled-up shoes, which had belonged to those or other prisoners; 3) a group of prisoners, still alive, seen behind a metal fence; 4) the 'death stairway' of 186 very high and irregular steps, which the forced laborers were made to climb under enormous loads right to the top, from which they were then often flung down into the pit below as a spectacle for the camp authorities; 5) a sentenced man on his knees before the ditch he himself has been made to dig, guarded by numerous German soldiers, one of whom is about to shoot him at the nape of the neck; 6) and a little series of frames (four in all) which show successive stages of a decompression-chamber experiment, performed on a human guinea pig.[27]

It will be forever impossible to know what poor illiterate Useppe may have understood of those meaningless photographs, writes Morante, but we, the readers, know. Here is a depiction of history in the years in which Useppe lived on this planet. The angel-like little happy child resembles the messiah which theology and political theory were looking for in their search of redemption, but *History* leaves no room for redemption. The little child accompanies the most horrible events with an innocent smile but manages to redeem nobody. Thus, it becomes much more difficult to walk the messianic route. Despite our Augustinian yearnings for the city of God, we are doomed, like Ida Ramundo, to live in history. This idea is put before us boldly and vigorously in the closing sentence of the novel: "and History continues...."[28]

Being There

In 1970, one decade before Ronald Reagan was elected president of the United States, two decades before Tony Blair was elected prime minister of Great Britain, and three decades before the practice of electing good-looking candidates for high office was no longer questioned anywhere in the world, Jerzy Kosinski composed the short novel *Being There* about an illiterate gardener who becomes a candidate for American vice president on the basis of his television skills. Kosinski was not endowed with prophetic vision. As an observer of social reality he identified the great power of television in modern politics and foresaw the rise to power of figures capable of utilizing that power, or who are manipulated by others who are. This novel joins a series of philosophical and literary critiques of modern democratic politics stressing the role of the mass media in its corruption.[1]

One needs to exercise some caution in the face of those often exaggerated critiques which relate to the mass media as an independent force that fundamentally changes all traditional democratic forms and processes. It is wrong to attribute omnipotent power to the mass media; democracy has often proven its viability against all odds.² On the other hand, large parts of the political game are nowadays conducted in the media. Political leaders are elected for high office while the voters have insufficient information about their character, skill, or political position.

Democracy has always been marked by the choice it provides between candidates. For instance, if *A* was a capitalist and *B* was a socialist, the two would spell out their competing ideologies to the electorate in order to get a mandate to rule in line with their respective preferences. But today this is no longer the case. In an election campaign taking place mainly before television cameras, the difference between *A* and *B* disappears. Both capitalists and socialists use slogans that appeal to large audiences. Ideological differences fade once the campaign is conducted by media experts, advertising firms, spokespersons, and copywriters who are naturally trying to reach the broadest common denominator. A political party aiming to win would discourage the ideologue and prefer the good-looking guy with the skill to appear healthy and wealthy – not necessarily wise – before the cameras.³

Kosinski deals with this phenomenon by taking it to an extreme. It is the story of an orphan living in the house of an old man, who may be his illegitimate father. He has been totally isolated from the outside world, his life limited to his quarters and to the garden. Besides a maid bringing him his food, he would meet nobody, just watch television. The author pictures him as fully integrated in the natural and virtual reality he is part of without an independent standing versus the garden or the television set. When he wonders in the garden, he never knows whether he is going forward or backward, whether he is ahead of or behind his previous steps. In other words, he moves in the rhythm of nature, and of television. He has no independent stature vis-à-vis the set but moves or does not move in its path; nothing changes for him besides the change of channels. As his only contact with the world is through images appearing and disappearing on the screen, his own being is described as self-created, like a TV image that floated into the world. Thus, his "real" being consists of being watched by others:

> When one was addressed and viewed by others, one was safe. Whatever one did would then be interpreted by the others in the

same way that one interpreted what they did. They could never know more about one than one knew about them.⁴

This means that people's existence depends on those watching them. The communication world created by Kosinski is one entirely dependent on floating images:

> As long as one didn't look at people, they did not exist. They began to exist, as on TV, when one turned one's eyes on them. Only then could they stay in one's mind before being erased by new images.⁵

In addition to this model of existing by nature of serving as an image for others, the author proposes a model of existence dependent on bureaucratic records. When the old man dies, and lawyers handling the estate investigate the gardener to discover who he is, they come to the conclusion that he does not exist because there is no record of him. Although he has a sense of being, of growing side by side with the trees in the garden, and of the change from the days of radio to that of color television with a remote control, the lawyers can find no trace of him as he possesses no checkbook, driver's license, medical insurance card, or birth certificate.

As in the story of Adam and Eve, the gardener is driven out of the house to never return. The doors and gate to the garden are locked and, walking for the first time in the sun, he is struck by a passing limousine. A woman in the limousine, EE, introduces herself, and although he has no name besides Chance, for he was born by chance, he recalls that in similar situations men on TV introduce themselves by two names and thus introduces himself as "Chance the gardener." EE understands "Chauncey Gardiner" and from that point onwards, the road to high office is paved, for the protagonist already possesses the right name, one that is easily absorbable by television audiences.

All of Chauncey Gardiner's responses, derived from TV, contribute to his political success. He has no life beyond the images he got from the screen and thus, in a world in which everybody is affected by television, Chauncey Gardiner turns into an admired figure. He has no language besides the language used on television, and that language is devoid of any unique ethnic or communal accent. His communication is perfect. When EE takes him to her house and they conduct a conversation, he repeats parts of her own sentences, as is done on TV, which cheers her up and makes her confident. When the president visits her ailing husband and Chance meets with him, he remembers that during televised press conferences, the president always looks straight at the viewers, and he therefore stares directly into his eyes. His hair glistening, his skin ruddy in his freshly pressed suit, Chance impresses men and women as only movie stars, or the politicians resembling them, do:

> Manly; well-groomed; beautiful voice; sort of a cross between Ted Kennedy and Cary Grant.[6]

Television provides Chance with an appearance of self-confidence and decency. He is never afraid of an uncertain future because on TV, the actors will always be there, everything has its sequel, and one just has to wait patiently for the next program. The decency stems from sexual morality on American TV. When EE makes love to Chance, he impresses her by his delicate approach learnt from a TV culture in which love-making involves a man and a women coming very close to each other, sometimes even partly undressed, but then the scene is obscured; a brand new image appears on the screen and the embrace of the man and woman is utterly forgotten.

Chauncey Gardiner's political success stems from three additional factors:

First, he has no past. As is well known, a person's past may often be a barrier, especially for politicians who are supposed to look pure and sinless:

> Gardiner has no background! And so he's not and cannot be objectionable to anyone! He's personable, well-spoken, and he comes across well on TV! And, as far as his thinking goes, he appears to be one of us.[7]

The gardener does not think at all, but he appears to be "one of us" because, since he lacks any existence beyond that projected by his audience, it is easy to project anything into him:

The people who watched him on their sets did not know who actually faced them; how could they, if they had never met him? ... Chance became only an image for millions of real people. They would never know how real he was, since his thinking could not be televised. And to him, the viewers existed only as projections of his own thought, as images. He would never know how real they were, since he had never met them and did not know what they thought.[8]

Second, his lack of awareness of the complexity of the world makes him voice a limited number of truisms, based on his experience in the garden, which are easily accepted by elites and masses alike. Statements like "There are spring and summer, but there are also fall and winter. And then spring and summer again"[9] are welcomed in a society preoccupied with complex problems which seem to have no solution. The solutions proposed in the public sphere seem complicated and are hard to implement. Thus, simple statements, based on gardening experience, raise hopes. When the president says they are the most refreshing and optimistic statements he has heard in a long time, he is probably right. In a world in which the complexity of the discourse on public problems does not assure their solution, simple statements are refreshing.

Third, Chauncey Gardiner is politically successful because the entire political system is perfectly adapted to the world of television. Politicians, diplomats, ambassadors, newspaper editors, reporters, producers, businessmen, secret service agents, and secretaries are attracted to Chauncey Gardiner because they themselves are engaged in virtual rather than real activities. When the only thing that matters is appearance, then the illiterate gardener with the perfect appearance is cherished. Had the system dealt with real issues – human welfare, avoidance of war, preservation of the environment, and the like – all the above actors would have had to be preoccupied with complex problem-solving. But when the essence of the game is preservation of one's power and status, mainly through frequent media appearances, then the illiterate gardener has an advantage. His illiteracy helps him flourish in the cocktail parties, talk shows, background discussions, small talk, and other symptoms of virtual politics.

In the modern political world, it has become customary to broadcast endless interviews with politicians while everybody – the interviewers, the interviewees, and the audience – is aware that nothing will be said. Under these circumstances, the gardener who has no comment on an article in the *New York Times* or declares he does not read newspapers at all because he is illiterate becomes very effective.

This book, then, may be seen as a satirical work on modern politics, mainly in the United States, where a person who is unknown may be elected, on the basis of television skills, to a position on which the fate of millions may depend. As in totalitarian states, where a cult of personality is built, the democratic system allows, according to this book, mass control by images. The book is often referred to when candidates appear on the political scene just because of the image they convey on television. For instance, on the eve of the 1996 presidential elections in the United States, former chief of staff Colin Powell, who considered joining the race, was compared to Chauncey Gardiner for his refusal to commit himself to any clear ideology. *Being There* is also referred to when grey, unknown candidates are proposed for high office, such as a supreme court justice, just because more capable candidates were rejected due to past scandals.

But the book is not only a political satire; it also makes a point – albeit not sufficiently developed – about the era of the 1960s during which it was written.

This was an era in which educated social groups in the capitalistic West reconsidered some of the foundations of the world they lived in, asking "who are we?" and "where are we going?" The students' rebellions in France, Germany, the United States, and elsewhere indicated that many young people in the modern industrial state were experiencing a feeling of suffocation. They felt they were losing their humanity in a setting dominated by omnipotent multinational corporations, bureaucratic organizations, and technological advances. And as was often the case when educated social groups lamented social and industrial progress, the solution was found in a return to nature. In the fashion of Rousseau and other romantics, revolutionary thinkers of the 1960s called for a return of civilization to the lost paradise of simplicity and purity, a return, in the language of this book, to the garden behind the wall surrounding the old man's house.

Kosinski hints at this romantic tendency in the emphasis given in the book to Krylov's fables. Chance cannot read and write but he impresses others because of his "Krylovian touch"[10] Krylov's fables are mostly concerned with human purity corrupted by complexity and modernity. Consider, for instance, the fable dealing with a simple, healthy, industrious gardener whose intellectual neighbor boasted he could grow better vegetables because of his use of scientific methods. In the end, no vegetables grew in the intellectual's garden while the simple man's garden flourished. Students of the 1960s, particularly in the United States, called for a return to Krylovian simplicity, to the formation of an America free of CIA, LBJ, imperialistic interests, gigantic corporations, and power brokers, a country nurturing true democracy, protecting the environment and getting out of Vietnam.

Although these claims were considered revolutionary at the time, they actually matched a profound American creed, namely, the belief that American capitalism grew as part of Americana and was deeply rooted in values related to land and nature. This is why an illiterate gardener could impress the American business community. Here is what EE's husband, the heavy capitalist, has to say when Chance, asked what business he is in, mentions the garden:

> A gardener! Isn't that the perfect description of what a real businessman is? A person who makes a flinty soil productive with the labor of his own hands, who waters it with the sweat of his own brow, and who creates a place of value for his family and for the community. Yes, Chauncey, what an excellent metaphor! A productive businessman is indeed a laborer in his own vineyard![11]

At the time the above claims were made, Kosinski was an American cultural hero who appeared frequently on television talk shows in a false identity.[12] Kosinski was born in 1933 to a Jewish family in Lodz, Poland, and spent the years of the Nazi occupation with his parents moving between shelters. After the war he studied in a Lodz high school as well as at the University of Warsaw and in 1957 was able to obtain a study visa in the United States. He studied at Columbia University, and a few months after his arrival received a generous grant from the CIA to write a book about the USSR, where he spent a year before his departure to America.

From here on, he began to invent a life story that turned him into a cultural hero. He made people believe that his bestseller *The Painted Bird*, about a child wandering alone in Nazi-occupied Poland during the war, was autobiographical; that his father, textile merchant, Mojzesz Lewinkopf, was a linguist and his mother – a pianist; that he had arrived in the United States with only $2.80 in his pocket (while in reality a $500 deposit was needed to obtain a study permit); that he escaped Poland by forging reference letters from fictitious figures (which was apparently not true), etc.

In 1982, when these facts were exposed in the *Village Voice*, and Kosinski was accused of plagiarizing *Being There*, America refused to believe it. Many, including the *New York Times*, defended him forcefully. But life under a partly invented identity finally took its toll. If Kosinski ever wrote an autobiography, it was *Being There*. Like Chauncey Gardiner, the author, who wandered with his parents during his adolescent years from shelter to shelter, did not have the opportunity to shape a "real" personality. Like his character, he found himself in the spotlight with his only identity being that projected by the cameras. *Being There*, it could be argued, is not the story of the manipulation of the masses by a sophisticated scoundrel but the tragic story of a man whose only identity is one that exists in the eyes of the watching public. The only time Chauncey Gardiner feels secure is when he watches television or is being watched on the screen. Whenever he finds himself in an uncertain situation, he turns on the TV and watches its "reassuring images."[13] As we can see when he engages in sexual relations, he is totally alienated from a world of human interactions.

Kosinski's point of view is thus one of alienation from the reality he observed in the 1960s, and this seemingly enabled him to expose the "deluxe alienation" of educated strata in the western world at the time. His philosophical argument is not stated clearly enough, but it may be reconstructed thus: Let us draw a model of the political world which the rebels of the 1960s, and American culture in general, long for. Let's draw the historical narrative differently, as if the warm, tribal, natural *Gemeinschaft* has not been replaced by the modern *Gesellschaft* existing in America. Let's picture a hypothetical, literary narrative in which the Garden of Eden was not abandoned for the sake of an industrial state with bureaucratic institutions, laws and regulations, social and occupational differentiation, diverse political interests, etc., but in which Rousseau's ideal has been implemented.

Rousseau expressed his loathing for complex civilization and his wish for a simple form of existence, and Chauncey Gardiner fulfills that wish. He has no documents, no address, no checkbook, he owns no driver's license and possesses no medial insurance card. He has never paid taxes, never gone to the dentist or the doctor, and never served in Vietnam. He is not a citizen of the state in the Aristotelian sense – he lacks any social affiliations or political interests and loyalties. He lives outside the time and space of the modern world. As we have seen, while in the garden he moved in consonance with the growing plants, and when he left the garden, he could continue to do so due to television in which there is no change of time and space, just the shifting of channels.

But the return of a complex society to nature, to a pre- or post-civilization existence, is dangerous. This can be seen as the main political message of the book. Kosinski, living in Poland during the Communist takeover, hated the Communist regime, which promised the masses a restoration of a paradise lost and subjected them instead to hunger, poverty, and political persecutions. America never did resemble, of course, this kind of totalitarianism, but Kosinski is concerned about the totalitarianism implied by a regime ruled by Chauncey Gardiner. A polity in which leadership is determined by televised images is undemocratic. It lacks political participation, the articulation and aggregation of diverse interests, and any form of political struggle. There are no failures and mishaps in that system, no wheeling and dealing, no negotiations, coalition building or recruitment of support, and there exist no moral dilemmas.

Chauncey Gardiner seems like a rather decent guy – he does not resemble any of the totalitarian leaders of the twentieth century. There is also a certain stability about him – he does not stagger back and forth between emotions. But there is no way to know how decent he is. In a moment of truth, when decision-makers decide the fate of other people's lives, a measure of human decency could make all the difference in the world. We have no way to tell how Chauncey Gardiner would behave at such a moment.

For one, he is not committed to truth, as the system described in the book has replaced truth by its appearance. Chauncey Gardiner lacks any mechanism of self-reflection and contemplation. He has no doubts or reservations, as there exist no objective standards against which one's acts may be evaluated. This, Kosinski tells us, is the mark of the age. In an age dominated by television, everything is invented anew every minute – there exist no stable norms that can be relied on. The television world consists of closed circles of images in which every occurrence is self-produced and all acts originate and end in virtual reality. The cyclical nature of the virtual world is illustrated when Chance discovers in a television studio that the cameras actually were not reflecting an external world but each other:

> Chance was astonished that television could portray itself; cameras watched themselves and, as they watched, they televised a program. This self-portrait was telecast on TV screens facing the stage and watched by the studio audience. Of all the manifold things that were in all the world – trees, grass, flowers, telephones, radios, elevators – only TV constantly held up a mirror to its own neither solid not fluid face.[14]

Such a cyclical system, avoiding contact with an external system of norms and possibly denying its existence, has grave political consequences.[15] When politics are played within a cycle of images, the distinction between good and bad is lost. In order to talk about a political act as good or bad, it must be set against a standard that not only exceeds the act itself but is rooted in a whole system of political restrictions, legal precedents, etc. In virtual politics, however, good acts are those that look good and bad acts are those that look bad.

Moreover, even when a bad act is exposed as such, its evil nature would soon be blurred in a flood of images, whether or not manipulated by the leadership. The phenomenon of political leaders caught in acts of corruption and similar felonies who, before hiring a lawyer, surround themselves with public relations experts is already a familiar one. These leaders will soon engage in endless television appearances intended to hide the felony under a pile of images that divert the attention of politicians, the legal system and the public to other matters. However confident Chauncey Gardiner seems to his viewers, the state Kosinski describes cannot be secure, as it has no historical past and no moral foundation. It lacks political commitment towards itself and towards others.

The undeniable power of television is brought to an extreme in this novel. Television has, of course, not only provided us with virtual images but has also brought previously ignored political facts, such as the facts of war, famine in remote regions, or political restlessness among previously ignored social groups, into our living rooms. Studies have shown that humans are exposed to the images portrayed by television in a more limited way than prophets of doom like Herbert Marcuse, Marshall McLuhan, or Neil Postman have predicted. The Aristotelian citizen belonging to a network of social groups engaged in communal political activity has not disappeared from the scene in the age of mass society. The increase in the power of the mass media and their owners has given rise to media-watch organizations and individual mechanisms providing protection from their overwhelming effect.

And yet, Kosinski's warning is in place. He warns us of the dangers involved in a direct jump from the old man's garden to the television studio, from nature to virtual reality, from one paradise to another. He warns us not to give up the intermediary stage of political civilization so despised by the rebels of the 1960s and by many today.

All over the world, a resentment of "politics as usual" is found in public opinion polls.[16] People resent the political process with its particularistic interests, endless conflicts, and ugly wheeling and dealing. They express fatigue with the long and tiring processes in which politicians engage in forming coalitions, negotiating compromises, and reaching consensus for policies. People are often willing to give up what seems like, and often is, a corrupt political process for a pure and clean virtual reality in which good-looking candidates provide, in straight talk, hope for "the future."

But what this means is giving up life in time and space, replacing reality by a cyclical, self-contained system of images whose main characteristic is a lack of commitment by any humans towards any other humans. *Being There* is a book about the abandonment of human interaction for the sake of a fascinating yet very dangerous adventure in which there is no failure but also no change and development. Chauncey Gardiner moves from success to success. He does not fail because his audience projects onto him its unrealistic hopes and desires. There is nothing he says that is not accepted because his laconic words do not endanger the continued existence of the virtual order.

Once in power, he could survive in office forever because he is not evaluated by any criteria but those that brought him to office in the first place. He is cherished by a society tired of complexity and disenchanted about its capacity to solve problems. His rise to power is aided by a lazy press unwilling to dig too hard into his background and by a phony elite, represented by EE, whose main interest lies in a smooth political process that would assure its own longevity. As EE says to the gardener she houses: "You're an angel, my dear. Thank God there are still men like you around to give aid and comfort."[17]

Jerzy Kosinski did not share EE's preferences. Although he himself became a TV star inventing a life story based on his audience's expectations, he probably realized the need of the individual for a life that is lived in separation from the cameras, to engage in human interactions, to develop and change, not just "being there." For on May 2, 1991, after coming home from a party where he performed, as usual, the celebrity role, he got into the bathtub and took his own life.

Being There, as well as the story of Kosinski's life – and death – may thus be seen above all as a story about the right of the individual to fail. Failure has never been desired in Western civilization. Educational systems, beginning in the home, socialize us to "succeed." The signals we detect throughout our life from parents, teachers, colleagues, and the mass media encourage us to "make it" in school, in sports, in our career, in our social life, in politics. "Nothing succeeds like success," the cliché goes, and very few dare object to it when planning their lives. Success is defined differently across cultures and periods, but it always includes a measure of appreciation by others. It is therefore intensely sought in politics. Political leadership is an indication of success and, at the same time, depends on the image of success.

As we follow Chauncey Gardiner making it to the top, we are filled with fear stemming not only from the gardener's illiteracy but from the nature of success. Kosinski brought the norm of success to the realm of the absurd, where it belongs. He demonstrated the shallowness involved in achieving social glamor and political power for its own sake. He made his protagonist climb the ladder only to reveal to the bystanders there is no human substance behind the role. He made us think more deeply about that substance than we usually do when we elect leaders and made us realize the place failure has, and ought to have, in our civilization. For it is in failure, not in success, that our human qualities are revealed, especially our compassion towards other humans. The successful leader has a good chance to fall into arrogance and vanity; the twentieth century has seen enormous destruction brought about by leaders pictured as larger than life who, convinced by the picture drawn of them, were willing to lead millions to their death.

Is there an alternative to choosing leaders by their proven and potential success? In his study of biblical leadership, theologian Martin Buber admitted that it is the moment of success that determines the selection of events that seem important to history. World history is the history of successes; in the heart of history only the conquerors have value. But the Bible, he wrote, knows nothing of this intrinsic value of success. On the contrary, when it announces a successful deed, it is duty-bound to announce in complete detail the failure involved in the success. Buber brings many examples – Moses who led the people out of Egypt but was defeated in every negotiation with them, King David who was not allowed to enjoy his triumphs, or the prophets whose existence was in failure throughout. Buber writes:

> This existence in the shadow, in the quiver, is the final word of the leaders in the biblical world; this enclosure in failure, in obscurity, even when one stands in the blaze of public life, in the presence of the whole national life. The truth is hidden in obscurity and yet does its work; though indeed in a way far different from that which is known and lauded as effective by world history.[18]

Chauncey Gardiner represents the exact opposite – there is neither truth nor real work hidden behind the appearance of success. Buber considered the biblical leaders as endowed not only with moral perfection but with a greater quality that stands at the center of his theology – the capacity to engage in genuine dialogue with God, nature, and other human beings. Chauncey Gardiner, on the other extreme, holds no dialogue – not even with himself. Thus, in a strange and complex way, this literary character joins in the great theologian's call to maintain the dialogical capacity, tamed by success but enhanced by failure, in public life.

Death of the Novel?

In *Shakespeare's Politics*, Allan Bloom writes that "the civilizing and unifying function of the peoples' books, which was carried out in Greece by Homer, Italy by Dante, France by Racine and Molière, and Germany by Goethe, seems to be dying a rapid death."[1] To Bloom, the failure of modern societies to return to single great books of biblical or Shakespearean stature leads to the vulgarization of public life and the atomization of society, "for a civilized people is held together by its common understanding of what is virtuous and vicious, noble and base."[2] I would like to agree with Bloom on the civilizing function of books without sharing his pessimism about their demise. Although it is not easy to derive a solid political theory from novels, whose analysis often leads to more remote venues than political theory tolerates, the twentieth-century novels discussed here serve as building blocks of a model of civil society.

This does not imply that these novels are *bildungsromane*,[3] that is, novels intended to convey an educational message. If anything, most of the novelists discussed here defy the conveyance of didactic messages and refrain from judgment of what is "virtuous and vicious, noble and base." The role these eight novels play as building blocks of the civil society model stems rather from the position the characters take in relation to the forces dominating the state and market in the twentieth century. They form a buffer against an overpowering discourse that places ideology, technology, and organization at center stage. All eight characters take part in that discourse but at the same time bring up facets of a model citizen who is conscious of his or her limitations, is aware of the need for social communication, seeks authenticity, refuses total political domination, uses reason, takes responsibility over acts committed by the state, views history as the product of human action rather than of messianic intervention, and maintains a degree of common decency in mass society.

The eight characters provide us with the discursive dimension between the market and the state sought by civil society theorists. They do so mainly by illuminating the world's imperfections, seen from their private sphere, in contrast to the loud promise of messianic redemption by the grand forces of the twentieth century. Hans Castorp reminds us that, even when humans use the power of science to play God, they remain mortal; Joseph K. makes us realize our helplessness in the face of bureaucracy; John the Savage embodies the search for authenticity in the modern industrial state; Winston Smith attempts to hold onto his memory when confronted by hegemonic political forces; Ralph is the voice of reason within the organic community; Meursault demands that we take responsibility for the atrocities of the age; Ida Ramundo reminds us there is no messiah at the end of the road; and Chauncey Gardiner demonstrates the high cost of mass society.

The vitality of these messages in today's world raises the possibility that they may not have been lost, as Bloom contends, with the alleged defeat of the novel by the power of electronic mass media; the announcement of the death of the novel may have been premature.

The argument that the novel is alive can be found in such works as Martha Nussbaum's *Poetic Justice*, where she defends the novel as a literary genre that has a strong impact on public life. In 1995, amidst criticism of the novel as reflecting the moral stand of a hegemony-seeking bourgeoisie, Nussbaum claimed that it still was the central morally serious yet popularly engaging fictional form of modern culture. She attributes this role to the novel's ability to present persistent forms of human need and desire in very concrete settings that sensitize readers to situations differing from their own:

> [The novel] constructs a paradigm of a style of ethical reasoning that is context-specific without being relativistic, in which we get potentially universizable concrete prescriptions by bringing a general idea of human flourishing to bear on a concrete situation, which we are invited to enter through the imagination. This is a valuable form of public reasoning, both within a single culture and across cultures. For the most part, the genre fosters it to a greater degree than classical tragic dramas, short stories, or lyric poems.[4]

Nussbaum admits that people cannot learn everything they need to learn as citizens simply by reading novels situated in a distant time and place, but the genre generally constructs empathy and compassion in ways highly relevant to citizenship. This theory of literary imagination as public imagination, and of the novel as a building block in the construction of citizenship, leaves many questions open: What about the apparent decline in the reading of books? Isn't the "public" watching television rather than reading novels? Hasn't the mass production and advertisement of "airport literature" led writers to avoid individual moral statements and to become disseminators of socially accepted conventions? Are the readers still sensitized to human needs and desires or have the mass media diminished such sensitivities? Is it legitimate to talk about novels as expressions of the human condition when there exists no cross-cultural agreement on that condition? And even when we read novels with empathy and compassion, isn't the world too complex to prevent their transference to other contexts, or to all contexts?

It is tempting to answer these questions by referring to book stores in Paris, New York, Delhi, Beijing, Prague, or Tel-Aviv, especially those open in the late evening hours, where one gets a different impression regarding the decline of the reading public, or children's sections in public libraries all over the world, where books are handled with reverence, or discussion groups and other activities initiated by bookstore chains like Barnes & Noble or Chapters, increasingly turning into centers of family and public outings, or virtual bookstores on the Internet, or statistics indicating a significant increase in book sales in recent years. But this would miss the point, just as studies announcing the death of the novel by reference to the high consumption of television or the impact of the Internet do. The question is not how many people, or what strata of the population, read novels, or how the consumption of novels compares to the consumption of other media, but where are conceptions relevant to the formation of citizenship derived from. And novels may still be playing an important role in this regard.

In a study titled *The Death of Literature*, Alvin Kernan viewed the novel as the product of the print culture whose demise can be expected in a television era. Although he admitted that there is no question of reading or printed materials disappearing, Kernan saw a contradiction between literature and television:

> At the deepest level the worldview of television is fundamentally at odds with the worldview of literature based on the printed book. As television watching increases, therefore, and more and more people derive, quite unconsciously, their sense of reality and their existential situation in it from television, the assumptions about the world that have been identified with literature will become less and less plausible, and in time will become downright incredible.[5]

To Kernan, the printed book with its intricacy of structure, complexity of meaning, irony, ambiguity, multivalency, and indeterminacy embodies the assumptions of an earlier humanism about such matters as truth, imagination, language, and history, while television creates a radically different way of seeing and interpreting the world:

> Visual images not words, simple open meanings not complex and hidden, transience not permanence, episodes not structures, theatre not truth. Literature's ability to coexist with television, which many take for granted, seems less likely when we consider that as readers turn into viewers, as the skill of reading diminishes, and as the world as seen through a television screen feels more and looks more pictorial and immediate, belief in a word-based literature will inevitably diminish.[6]

Although this notion is widespread, it has not been proven that people are giving up the means by which they confront the world and make sense of it. The means of communication may be changing but not the need, which existed long before print culture and can be expected to exist long after its transformation into different cultural modes, to derive meaning about the world, and negotiate one's existence, as perceived in any given time, with others. It has become commonplace to lament the mixture of "high" and "popular" culture," caused by twentieth-century urbanization and democratization, as a decline of civilization into a normless mass, but this lament has been highly exaggerated. Young people attracted to rock concerts rather than to Shakespearean dramas, or people who prefer to receive quick, instant information from television or the Internet rather than from a lecture in a book club, are not necessarily changing from humanists into savages lacking a sense of truth, imagination, language, and history. As William Gamson has shown in a study on the consumption of political messages on television, people are much less passive and stupid than media researchers have assumed and are conducting elaborate and complex negotiations with the contents presented in the mass media.[7]

Despite their cultural and political differentiation, today's members of mass society do not differ from the idealized citizens of the past in their need to formulate conceptions of public significance and, just like them, they do not develop these conceptions only as actors in the market or as subjects of the state. Nor can they be seen to be influenced merely by the mass media they consume. The individual who steps into a government office develops awareness about the way individuals are treated there, and about the dissonance between the actual and desired treatment – residing at the core of political theory – as part of a complex process in which novels can be assumed to take part by virtue of their adherence to the private sphere. Novels reflect individual thoughts and feelings in a personalized way which mass media, especially radio call-in shows and television talk shows, imitate but, as has often been revealed, really only appear to.[8]

Even a person who is rather conditioned in his or her responses to public affairs by such genres as daytime soap operas cannot entirely avoid the presence of novels. This is because of the convergence that characterizes today's media structures; the novel, the movie, the T-shirt, the theme ride, the video game, etc., are all converging into one media world.[9] The novel may be affected by the convergence, but so is the soap opera, which adopts forms and themes derived from novels, such as the narrative, the moral imperative, or the need to make individual choices at critical moments. In fact, the novel, like other traditional media, seems to have more power than commonly realized to reinvent itself and become a factor in the public sphere.

The taxi driver complaining about the "red tape" involved in applying for a cab license does not have to be tested for his acquaintance with Kafka in order to be classified as a citizen engaged in a public discourse whose parameters were largely defined by the novelist. Kafka did not invent modern bureaucracy and was not the first to express fear of its power and awareness of its flaws. More people are exposed to bureaucratic maneuvering on television police and hospital dramas than have read *The Trial*. But Kafka's books inspired the thinking of whole generations about bureaucracy, including, one may assume, creators of television dramas.

As little as we know about the process of inspiration, influential books in the public domain were often those that cater to a third dimension of public life independent of commercial and political interests. The notion of "big brother" in George Orwell's *1984*, for instance, has great influence on the thinking of many, not only because Orwell provided a convenient language to describe the modern political condition, but because he penetrated that condition in a depth that other media have so far rarely matched. How the notion of "big brother," with its varied meanings and interpretations, is diffused through culture, or cultures, and becomes a component of the public consciousness is of course hard to trace; the formation of the public consciousness remains as much a secret as the formation of the individual mind. But *1984*, or for that matter, some of the other novels we discussed, became quite famous among the millions who read the books, or saw the movies, or read about them in newspapers and magazines, or heard something about them, or use expressions derived from them.

As I noted before, the diffusion of novels within and across media systems and cultures in relation to other literary genres and media is hard to trace, but a closer investigation of the diffusion of conceptions derived from novels may reveal their persistent role in maintaining a standard of civility in society. In a world in which much human interaction takes place within bureaucratic and legal structures, in which many media professionals, intellectuals, educators, and other communicators have given up on their traditional promise to provide a rational flow of information in society, and in which "enlightenment" has become a bad word concealing suppressive and exclusionist motives, novels remain among the few means by which notions of global citizenship are promoted.

This contention calls for a revival of Jürgen Habermas's widely criticized notion of the "public sphere." In *The Structural Transformation of the Public Sphere*, he pointed to "a theater in modern societies in which political participation is enacted through the medium of talk."[10] The public sphere as the discursive arena of civil society emerged as part of the development of the European bourgeoisie. The liberalization of the market since the High Middle Ages, writes Habermas, has allowed the crystallization of civil society as a private realm, a process enhanced by new media, such as the newspaper and the literary salon, which allowed individuals to engage in issues beyond those desired by economic patrons, church patriarchs, and state leaders.

One of the main media that in Habermas's view enhances the public sphere is literary fiction. It is therefore no wonder it became a central target of his critics. Locating the private sphere mainly in the bourgeois household, Habermas emphasized literary fiction as the expression of the private consumed in public. In the intimate sphere of the conjugal family, he wrote, privatized individuals developed the conception of the person who is independent even from economic activity and is capable of purely human relations with others. The literary forms that expressed this conception was the letter – the expression of subjective feelings to an audience – and the novel which is an extension of the letter:

> On the one hand, the empathetic reader repeated within himself the private relationships displayed before him in literature; from his experience of real familiarity (*Intimität*), he gave life to the fictional one, and in the latter he prepared himself for the former. On the other hand, from the outset the familiarity (*Intimität*) whose vehicle was the written word, the subjectivity that had become fit to print, had in fact become the literature appealing to a wide public of readers. The privatized individuals coming together to form a public also reflected critically and in public on what they had read, thus contributing to the process of enlightenment which they together promoted.[11]

In Habermas's theory, the demise of the public sphere in the late nineteenth century is strongly tied to the decline of the reading public. He laments the replacement of the "public sphere in the world of letters" by a "pseudo-public or sham-private world of cultural consumption."[12] While admitting that systems of mass distribution of books, such as paperback editions and book clubs, expose pupils, students, and others to the literary treasures previously open only to the few, he relates the modern culture of book consumption to the destruction of the public sphere. Consumerism does not go hand in hand with genuine literary critique, and the broadening of the reading public to include almost all strata of the population is no reason to rejoice, as it does not reflect the actual prevalence of book reading.

If in the past, the reading of novels and the writing of letters were preconditions for participation in the public sphere, he believes that since the late nineteenth century this is no longer so. The mass media cannot replace the literary public sphere as the world fashioned by them is a public sphere in appearance only. Even when the mass media adopt traditional literary terms (e.g., the "news story"), they blur the relationship between the private and public realms by portraying in public a fake intimacy:

> The original relationship of the domain of interiority to the public sphere in the world of letters is reversed. An inner life oriented toward a public audience tends to give way to reifications related to the inner life.[13]

The apparent decline of the novel as a source of public discourse did not seem to worry critics who treated the novel as a major component of the exclusionist culture dominating the public sphere. George Yúdice used particularly harsh words:

> The public sphere celebrated by Habermas, in which there was "no authority beside that of the better argument" was founded, as he himself recognizes, on the authority of patriarchy (and we should add class privilege, racism, and colonialism). That is, the "public" presupposed a sphere of privacy rooted in the patriarchal conjugal family. On this account, the novel emerged as the aesthetic form that publicly represented subjectivity as "the innermost core of

the private." This grounding for the public/private divide had, of course, changed. And the novel, an art form rooted in bourgeois institutions, is no longer the form through which the hegemonic totality of the social formation is inscribed in the constitution of the subjectivity. On the contrary, the novel, like autobiography and the diary, is used by subaltern groups to construct particular rather than overarching hegemonic identities.[14]

Having abolished the possibility that novels address the entire social formation, Yúdice goes on to search for "an aesthetic dimension that can contribute to change across the terrain of the social formation."[15] He believes this search could be successful if the aesthetic were understood "outside of the dominant accounts of autonomy in which it has been straitjacketed throughout modernity,"[16] that is, if literature and other forms of art are conceived as means in the formation of group identity and ethos. He falls short of explaining why aesthetic forms could not be conceived as means in the formation of a universal identity and ethos.

In a study on American fiction, religion, and the public sphere, Robert Detweiler hinted at that possibility by claiming that the novel, although rooted in bourgeois institutions, never was the unadulterated voice or efficient instrument of hegemony but rather criticized its own social-political conditions from the very start. Moreover, even novelists engaged in "counter discourses"[17] participate through their involvement in the politics and economics of commercial publishing in creating and producing a majority discourse. It is hard not to agree with Detweiler's conclusion that "the language of postbourgeois theory about the public realm is not adequate to treat the complications of the relationship of literary (and dramatic and cinematic) fiction to public discourse."[18]

Along the same lines, Nicholas Garnham, in a book that is otherwise critical of Habermas, writes:

> If we accept that the economic system is indeed global in scope and at the same time crucially determining over large areas of social action, the Enlightenment project of democracy requires us to make a Pascalian bet on universal rationality. For without it the

project is unrealizable, and we will remain in large part enslaved to a system outside our control.[19]

Struggling with the question of whether the Enlightenment project is possible at all, Garnham transfers the question from the realm of the polemic to that of the empirical:

> Only history will show whether the project is in fact realizable. The possibility of arriving at a rationally grounded consensus can only be demonstrated in practice by entering into a concrete and historically specific process of rational debate with other human beings on the assumption that the system world is at least partially subjectable to rational control, that it is in the ultimate interest of most human beings so to control it, that other human beings can be led both to a rational recognition of that interest within a common discourse space and to consensual agreement as to the appropriate cooperative courses of action to follow.[20]

These words serve as an important reminder that recent intellectual notions emphasizing ethnic, cultural, and gender distinctions need not nullify the Pascalian wager, and that the urge to maintain the Enlightenment project, whether or not the term is capitalized, can be motivated by a genuine quest for autonomy from the power of the state and the forces of the market. Such temporary and tentative removal of the claim that the public sphere is related, in principle, to a domineering wish allows a self-confident renewal of the search for universal rationality and a consideration of the novel carrying with it greater self-confidence than the "Death of Literature" theory has allowed so far.

In considering the contribution of the novel to universal, rational public discourse, we must be careful not to romanticize it. Most novels sold in bookstores do not differ from other means of communication in their adherence to the rules of the market. Novels, like other media, are often shallow and boring, too long or too short, and written in accordance with passing literary fashions. Novels may fake what seems like intimate privacy no less than radio and television do. The very reluctance of many to read novels is of course a hindrance to their impact, and movies or television broadcasts occasionally send very effective messages that books cannot compete with.

What differentiates novels from other media, however, is the fact that some of them are unmatched in the discreet yet deep penetration they provide into another individual's private sphere. When we hold a novel that caught our attention in our hands, in an armchair or in bed, when we spend several hours reading it, we have a unique experience in which an intimate dialogue, matched perhaps only by poetry, takes place between two strangers, who would in most cases remain strangers. Novels endow us with a form of enlightenment unmatched even by face-to-face communication. It is not that a face-to-face meeting with Thomas Mann could not be enlightening – it definitely was to those who met him during his lifetime – but it is through our meeting with Hans Castorp that the private sphere of the writer becomes part of our consciousness.

The role of novels in our lives may have a deeper cognitive function than we used to believe. In his excellent study on the development of information technologies mentioned before, Wade Rowland compares the cognitive skills involved in reading books and watching television. Reading books – and to some extent watching cinema – involves literacy, imagination, and interpretive skills, while television asks only that the viewer show up and it will do the rest; even laughter is supplied. Civility and erudition are not effective, for aggressive confrontation is preferred. This is related to the different areas of the brain affected by the respective media:

> Whereas a book, for example, engages us through our intellect, television acts directly on our neuromuscular system. Each rapid-fire edit, each "jolt" provided by TV, sets up in our bodies what is known in clinical psychology as an "orientation response." This subliminal reaction, which can be monitored with the appropriate equipment, prepares us to either examine the object or event or withdraw from it. Clinical observation has determined that it takes, on average, about half a second for an individual to absorb the nature of the "occurrence" and decide how to react. In making that response decision, the tension of the "orientation response" is resolved. Television, De Kerckhove and others have argued, is designed to deny its audience that half-second response time and

the subsequent resolution, and thus to maintain a high level of tension in which rational thought is suppressed.[21]

This points at the capacity of television to communicate directly through the body rather than the intellect, which affects the messages conveyed by each medium. Many studies have shown how unsubtle and unsophisticated television images are. In one study, the sophisticated treatment of human destiny in novels is compared to the simple moralism in the mass media. Wilna Meijer expresses the concern of cultural pessimists over the decline of reading and sees its consequence mainly to the abandonment of the sense of tragedy in human affairs. Through art, she writes, we gain insight into human beings – not by general abstraction, but because art imitates the human condition in concrete, ever-varying webs of circumstances. Ethical, practical understanding feeds on concrete detailed stories rather than on general principles and rules. Her main example of ethical understanding based on concrete stories are Greek tragedies whose readers learn about the many ways in which human beings, despite their good intentions, get entangled in unforeseen situations. Moralizing, on the other hand, reduces such situations to simple causal relations between intention and result, based on apriori generalizations. She therefore concludes, after Kundera, that the novel comes closer to human and humane truth than the mass media since it prompts its readers "to suspend judgement, to discover things are ever more complex than they appeared at first sight, and to accept that ambiguity may have the final say."[22]

Rather than catering to cultural pessimists, the distinction between the cognitive processes related to novels and to television raises the possibility that even television edicts are at one point or another in need of the structural and substantive features found in novels. In *The Triumph of Narrative* Robert Fulford cites studies in various areas considering these features as functional to human development. Anthropologist Clifford Geertz believes that humans are symbolizing, conceptualizing, meaning-seeking animals possessed by a drive as pressing as more familiar biological needs to make sense out of experience and to give it form and order. Ethical philosopher Alasdair MacIntyre says that humans create their sense of what matters, and how they should act, by referring consciously or unconsciously to the stories they have learned which constitute important dramatic resources. And language and cognitive scientist Mark Turner argues that telling stories is not a luxury or a pastime but part of developing intelligence. Stories are the building blocks of human thought, they are the way the brain organizes itself.[23]

This is not to say of course that all novels or their characters affect us in similar fashion. Some characters speak to us more than others. Some attract us, others repel us and still others remain a placard. We may feel ambivalence towards them and the world they represent. But individuals, including many who declare they never have time to read books, have an image of literary figures they encountered either directly or indirectly through reviews, conversations, movie productions, etc. What makes these literary characters important is their residence in the public consciousness as private people. Whether romantic heroes serving the nation-state, ideological heroes encouraging commitment to collective goals, or twentieth-century characters attempting to cope with messianic politics, they do so as individuals whose private sphere is exposed to us to internalize and reflect upon. Novels mostly do not affect political action in any visible way, but they provide a handle for individuals to hold onto when they observe political processes and – as was the case in the twentieth century – are overwhelmed by them.

The political insights conveyed by the eight novels analyzed here are obviously not the only ones found in twentieth-century novels. Different insights may even be derived from those eight novels. The civil message underlying them is however worth noting if only because of the hope it entails. It is the hope that individualism may survive the hardest challenges. For the challenge posed to individualism in the twentieth century was unbearable. Not only did the forces of ideology, technology, and organization take over, while doing so they endowed themselves with a messianic promise for the transcendence of history, which hardly left any chance to Hans Castorp, Joseph K., John the Savage, Winston Smith, Ralph, Meursault, Ida Ramundo, and Chauncey Gardiner. And yet, the presence of these characters in our public consciousness, and the message of civility they convey, assure us that, as long as the political novel does not give in to other mass media, a touch of civility may continue to accompany us in the future.

Notes

Notes to Introduction

1. See Evans Lansing Smith, *The Hero Journey in Literature: Parables of Poesis* (Lanham, MD: University Press of America, 1997).
2. John Richetti, "The Novel and Society: The Case of Daniel Defoe." In *The Idea of the Novel in the Eighteenth Century*, Robert W. Uphaus, ed. (East Lansing, MI: Colleagues Press, 1988), p. 50.
3. Walter L. Reed, *Meditations on the Hero: A Study of the Romantic Hero in Nineteenth-Century Fiction* (New Haven, CT: Yale University Press, 1974).
4. See David Bruce Suchoff, *Critical Theory and the Novel: Mass Society and Cultural Criticism in Dickens, Melville, and Kafka* (Madison: University of Wisconsin Press, 1994).
5. See James Swift, *Civil Society in Question* (Toronto: Between the Lines, 2000).
6. See Ralf Dahrendorf, *Reflections on the Revolution in Europe*.(London: Chatto & Windus, 1990); Percy B. Lehring "Toward a Multicultural Civil Society: The Role of Social Capital and Democratic Citizenship." *Government and Opposition* 33 (spring 1998): 221–42.
7. On the history of the term, see Dominique Colas, *Civil Society and Fanaticism: Conjoined Histories* (Stanford: Stanford University Press, 1997).
8. Michael Walzer "The Civil Society Argument." In *Theorizing Citizenship*, Ronald Beiner, ed. (Albany: State University of New York Press, 1995).
9. Benjamin R. Barber, *Jihad vs. McWorld* (New York: Random House, 1995), p. 284.
10. Ibid., p. 285.
11. Ibid., p. 286.
12. Mark Kingwell, *The World We Want: Virtue, Vice and the Good Citizen* (Toronto: Penguin, 2000), p. 56.
13. See: David Caute, *The Fellow Travellers: Intellectual Friends of Communism* (New Haven, CT: Yale University Press, 1988).
14. Jeffrey C. Goldfarb, *Civility and Subversion: The Intellectual in Democratic Society* (Cambridge: Cambridge University Press, 1998), p. 123.
15. Christopher Hitchens, *Acknowledged Legislation: Writers in the Public Sphere* (London: Verso, 2000), p. xiv.
16. Ibid.
17. Milan Kundera, "Jerusalem Address: The Novel and Europe." In *The Art of the Novel*, Milan Kundera, ed. (New York: Grove Press, 1988), p. 164.
18. Irving Howe, *Politics and the Novel* (New York: Horizon, 1957), p. 17.
19. Paul A. Cantor, "Literature and Politics; Understanding the Regime." *PS: Political Science and Politics* 28 (June 1995): 193.
20. *The World We Want*, p. 116.
21. Plato, *Complete Works*, John M. Cooper, ed. (Indianapolis: Hacket, 1997), p. 1017.
22. Paul J. Dolan, *Of War and War's Alarms: Fiction and Politics in the Modern World* (New York: Free Press, 1976), p. 3.

23 John Horton and Andrea T. Baumeister, "Literature, Philosophy and Political Theory." In *Literature and the Political Imagination*, John Horton and Andrea T. Baumeister, eds. (London: Routledge, 1996), p. 12.
24 Ibid., p. 13.
25 John Horton, "Life, Literature and Ethical Theory: Martha Nussbaum on the Role of the Literary Imagination in Ethical Thought." In *Literature and the Political Imagination*, p. 78.
26 Susan Mendus, "'What of Soul Was Left, I Wonder?': The Narrative Self in Political Philosophy." In *Literature and the Political Imagination*, p. 59.
27 Catherine Zuckert, "Why Political Scientists Want to Study Literature," *PS: Political Science & Politics* 29 (1995): 189–90.

Notes to We Are Not Immortal
1 Paul Johnson, *A History of the Modern World: From 1917 to the 1980s* (London: Weidenfeld and Nicolson, 1983), p. 11.
2 Stefan Zweig, *The World of Yesterday: An Autobiography* (London: Cassell, 1987), p. 32.
3 Michael Harrington, *The Accidental Century* (New York: Macmillan, 1965), p. 44.
4 Ibid.
5 Katia Mann, *Meine Ungeschriebene Memoiren* (Frankfurt: Fischer, 1974).
6 See Harold Bloom, ed., *Thomas Mann's The Magic Mountain* (New York: Chelsea, 1986).
7 Thomas Mann, *The Magic Mountain* (New York: Knopf, 1960), p. V. (I have used throughout the translation into English by H.T. Lowe-Porter.)
8 Ibid., p. 4.
9 Ibid.
10 See Hugo G. Walter, *Space and Time on the Magic Mountain: Studies in Nineteenth and Early Twentieth-Century European Literature* (New York: Peter Lang, 1999); Michael Bell, *Literature, Modernism and Myth: Belief and Responsibility in the Twentieth Century* (Cambridge: Cambridge University Press, 1997).
11 See Hermann J. Weigand, *The Magic Mountain: A Study of Thomas Mann's Novel Der Zauberberg* (Chapel Hill: University of North Carolina Press, 1965).
12 *The Magic Mountain*, p. 262.
13 Ibid., p. 266.
14 Ibid.
15 Ibid.
16 Ibid.
17 Frederick Neuhouser, *Foundations of Hegel's Social Theory: Actualizing Freedom* (Cambridge, MA: Harvard University Press, 2000).
18 *The Magic Mountain*, p. 274.
19 Kenneth Thompson, ed., *Auguste Comte: The Foundation of Sociology* (London: Nelson, 1976), p. 39.
20 Ibid., p. 40.
21 Alan Swingewood, "Industrialization and the Rise of Sociological Positivism." In *Early Modern Social Theory: Selected Interpretive Readings*, Murray E.G. Smith, ed. (Toronto: Canadian Scholars' Press, 1998): 74–99.
22 Gianfranco Poggi, *Durkheim* (Oxford: Oxford University Press, 2000), p. 7.

23 Ibid., p. 10.
24 Jacques Barzun, *From Dawn to Decadence: 1500 to the Present* (New York: Harper Collins, 2000), p. 652.
25 Ibid., p. 767.
26 *The Magic Mountain*, p. 244.
27 Ibid., p. 245.
28 Ibid., pp. 245–46.
29 Karl Mannheim, *Ideology and Utopia* (New York: Harcourt, 1936).
30 *The Magic Mountain*, p. 270.
31 Richard Tarnas, *The Pasion of the Western Mind: Understanding the Ideas that Have Shaped Our World View* (New York: Ballantine Books, 1991).
32 Ibid., p. 329.
33 Carl E. Schorske, *Fin-de-Siècle Vienna: Politics and Culture* (New York: Vintage, 1961), p. 203.
34 Thomas Mann, "Freud and the Future." In *Death in Venice, Tonio Kröger and Other Writings*, Frederick A. Lubich, ed. (New York: Continuum, 1999), p. 295.
35 Ibid.
36 Ibid., p. 296.
37 Quoted in James William Anderson and Jerome A. Winer, eds., "Introduction." *Annual of Psychoanalysis* 29 (2001): 4.
38 Ibid.
39 John F. Kihlstrom, "Is Freud Still Alive? Not Really." http://socrates.berkeley.edu/~kihlstrm/freuddead.htm
40 *The Magic Mountain*, p. 126.
41 Ibid.
42 Ibid., p. 127.
43 Ibid., p. 130.
44 Ibid., p. 215.
45 Ibid., p. 214.
46 Ibid.
47 Ibid., p. 215.
48 Ibid., p. 216.
49 Ibid., p. 218.
50 Ibid.
51 Anthony Heilbut, *Thomas Mann: Eros and Literature* (New York: Knopf, 1996).
52 *The Magic Mountain*, pp. 398–99.
53 Ibid., p. 399.
54 Ibid., p. 400.
55 Ibid.
56 Ibid., p. 469.
57 Ronald N. Stromberg, *Redemption by War: The Intellectuals and 1914* (Lawrence, KS: The Regents Press of Kansas, 1982).
58 Martha Hanna, *The Mobilization of Intellect: French Scholars and Writers during the Great War* (Cambridge, MA: Harvard University Press, 1996), p. 21.
59 *The Magic Mountain*, p. 714.

Notes to A Bureaucratic Nightmare

1. S.N. Eisenstadt, ed., *Max Weber on Charisma and Institution Building* (Chicago: University of Chicago Press, 1968), p. 70.
2. Ibid., p. 67.
3. Ibid., pp. 67–68.
4. Ibid., p. 68.
5. Ibid.
6. Ibid., p. 75.
7. Ibid.
8. Ronald Hayman, *K: A Biography of Kafka* (London: Weidenfeld and Nicolson, 1981), p. 69.
9. Quoted in ibid., p. 70.
10. Johannes Urzidil, *The Living Contribution of Jewish Prague to Modern German Literature* (New York: Leo Baeck Institute, 1968), p. 8.
11. *The Diaries of Franz Kafka 1914–1923* (New York: Schocken, 1949), pp. 75–77.
12. George Steiner, "Our Homeland the Text." *Salmagundi* 66 (winter–spring 1985): 13.
13. Jane Bennett, "Deceptive Comfort: The Power of Kafka's Stories." *Political Theory* 19 (February 1991): 73–95.
14. Franz Kafka, *The Trial* (New York: Schocken, 1992), p. 1.
15. Ibid., p. 4.
16. Ibid., p. 3.
17. Ibid., p. 6.
18. Ibid., p. 3.
19. Ibid., p. 5–6.
20. Ibid., p. 12.
21. Ibid., pp. 45–46.
22. Ibid., p. 34.
23. Ibid., p. 63.
24. Ibid., p. 146.
25. Ibid., p. 108.
26. Ibid., p. 150.
27. Ibid., p. 121.
28. Ibid., p. 226.
29. Ibid., p. 58.
30. Ibid. pp 58–59.
31. Ibid., p. 92.
32. Ibid., p. 70.
33. Ibid., p. 113.
34. William H. Whyte, Jr., *The Organization Man* (New York: Simon and Schuster, 1956), pp. 3–4.
35. Ibid., p. 404.
36. John Kenneth Galbraith, *The New Industrial State* (Boston: Houghton Mifflin, 1971), p. 372.
37. Peter F. Drucker, *Managing in a Time of Great Change* (New York: Truman Talley, 1995), p. 17.

Notes to In Quest of Authenticity

1. Kenneth E. Boulding, *The Meaning of the Twentieth Century: The Great Transition* (New York: Harper & Row, 1964).
2. John Kenneth Galbraith, *The New Industrial State* (New York: New American Library, 1978).
3. Jacques Ellul, *The Technological Society* (New York: Vintage, 1964), p. 6.
4. Alvin Toffler, *Future Shock* (New York: Random House, 1970).
5. Ralph E. Lapp, *The New Priesthood: The Scientific Elite and the Uses of Power* (New York: Harper & Row, 1965).
6. Aldous Huxley, *Brave New World* (London: Granada, 1977), p. 15.
7. Ibid.
8. Ibid., p. 7.
9. Ibid., p. 96.
10. Harold H. Watts, *Aldous Huxley* (New York: Twayne, 1969), p. 77.
11. Ibid., pp. 78–79.
12. *Brave New World*, p. 40.
13. Ibid., p. 196.
14. Ibid., p. 197.
15. Ibid., p. 44.
16. Ibid., pp. 44.
17. Ibid., p. 49.
18. Aldous Huxley, "Education for Freedom." In *Brave New World Revisited*. Aldous Huxley, ed. (London: Chatto & Windus, 1958), p. 144.
19. Aldous Huxley, "Chemical Persuasion." In *Brave New World Revisited*, op. cit., p. 100.
20. Aldous Huxley, Brave New World, op. cit., p. 78.
21. Ibid., p. 80.
22. Ibid., p. 75.
23. See Jack Nelson-Pallmeyer, *Brave New World: Must We Pledge Allegiance?* (Maryknoll, NY: Orbis, 1992).
24. *Brave New World*, p. 179.
25. Ibid., p. 47.
26. Barbara Tuchman: *The March of Folly; From Troy to Vietnam* (New York: Ballantine, 1985).
27. Wade Roland, *Spirit of the Web: The Age of Information from Telegraph to Internet* (Toronto: Key Porter, 1999), p. 93.

Notes to Resisting Big Brother

1. See Abbott Gleason, *Totalitarianism: The Inner History of the Cold War* (New York: Oxford University Press, 1995).
2. See Hannah Arendt, *The Origins of Totalitarianism* (New York: Meridian, 1951).
3. See Carl Friedrich and Zbigniew Brzezinski, *Totalitarian Dictatorship and Autocracy* (Cambridge, MA: Harvard University Press, 1965).
4. See J. L. Talmon, *The Origins of Totalitarian Democracy* (London: Secker and Warburg, 1952).
5. See Alok Rai, *Orwell and the Politics of Despair* (Cambridge: Cambridge University Press, 1988); John Newsinger, *Orwell's Politics* (New York: St. Martin's Press, 1999).

6   See Irving Howe, ed., *1984 Revisited: Totalitarianism in Our Century* (New York: Harper & Row, 1983); George Woodcock, *Orwell's Message: 1984 and the Present* (Madeira Park, B.C.: Harbour, 1984).
7   See Michael Sheldon, *Orwell: The Authorized Biography* (London: Heinemann, 1991).
8   George Orwell, *1984* (New York: The New American Library, 1961 [1949]), p. 222.
9   Ibid., p. 100.
10 Ibid., p. 11.
11 Ibid., pp. 128–29.
12 Ibid., p. 16.
13 Ibid., p. 19.
14 Ibid., p. 28.
15 Ibid., pp. 107–9.
16 Ibid., p. 13.
17 Ibid.
18 Ibid., p. 53.
19 *1984*, p. 169.
20 Thomas W. Cooper, "Fictional 1984 and Factual 1984." In *The Orwellian Moment: Hindsight and Foresight in the Post-1984 World*, Robert L. Savage et al., eds. (Fayetteville: University of Arkansas Press, 1989), p. 91.
21 Ibid., p. 26.
22 Ibid., p. 37.
23 See discussion on the matter in Howard J. Shaffer et al., "'Computer Addiction': A Critical Consideration." *American Journal of Orthopsychiatry* 70 (April 2000): 162–67. 174 Tim Cavanaugh, "Let Slip the Blogs of War." In *USC Annenberg Online Journalism Review*.
25 See: Steven Seidman, *Contested Knowledge: Social Theory in the Postmodern Era* (Malden: Blackwell, 1998).
26 Pauline Marie Rosenau, *Post-Modernism and the Social Sciences* (Princeton: Princeton University Press, 1992).
27 Keith Windschuttle, *The Killing of History: How Literary Critics and Social Theorists are Murdering Our Past* (New York: The Free Press, 1996), p. 2.
28 *1984*, p. 69.
29 Ibid., p. 30.
30 James Q. Wilson, "The Drama of the College Wars." *Academic Questions* 6 (fall 1993): 13.
31 Gorman Beauchamp, "Orwell, The Lysenko Affair, and the Politics of Social Construction." *Partisan Review* 68 (2000): 268.
32 Diane Ravitch, "Education after the Culture Wars." *Daedalus* (summer 2002), p. 5.
33 Ibid., p. 20.
34 TRC Report: http://www.jutastat.com/products/southafrican/trcr.htm
35 George Orwell, "Inside the Whale." In *Inside the Whale and Other Essays* (Harmondsworth: Penguin, 1962), p. 17.
36 George Orwell, *Homage to Catalonia* (London: Secker & Warburg, 1951), p. 18.
37 George Orwell, "Looking Back on the Spanish War." *Collected Essays* (London: Secker & Warburg, 1961), p. 204.
38 Ibid., p. 205.
39 Ibid., p. 217.

Notes to No Fire; No Smoke; No Rescue

1. See James R. Baker, "William Golding: Three Decades of Criticism." In *Critical Essays on William Golding*, James R. Baker, ed. (Boston: G. K. Hall, 1988): 1–11.
2. Virginia Tiger, *William Golding* (London: Calder and Boyars 1974).
3. See Patrick Reilly, *The Literature of Guilt: From Gulliver to Golding* (Iowa City: University of Iowa Press, 1988).
4. William Golding, *Lord of the Flies* (New York: Capricorn, 1959), p. 170.
5. Ibid., p. 5.
6. Ibid., p. 8.
7. Ibid., p. 33.
8. Ibid., p. 20.
9. Ibid., p. 72.
10. Ibid., p. 180.
11. Ibid., p. 72.
12. Ibid., p. 113.
13. Ibid., p. 28.
14. Ibid., p. 59.
15. Ibid., p. 59.
16. Ibid., p. 120.
17. Ibid., pp. 38–39.
18. Ibid., p. 144.
19. See Ruth Ben-Ghiat, *Fascist Modernists: Italy 1922–1945* (Berkeley: University of California Press, 2001).
20. See Paul Hollander, *Political Pilgrims: Travels of Western Intellectuals to the Soviet Union, China and Cuba 1928–1978* (New York: Oxford University Press, 1981).
21. See Paul Johnson, *Intellectuals* (London: Weidenfeld and Nicolson, 1988). Chapter 9.
22. See George Orwell, "Inside the Whale" In *Inside the Whale and Other Essays* (Harmondsworth: Penguin, 1962).
23. See Klaus-Georg Riegel, "Divided Community: East German Socialist Intellectuals and their Attitudes towards the Reunification of West Germany." *Development and Society* 31 (June 2002): 53–78.
24. Mark Lilla, *The Reckless Mind: Intellectuals in Politics* (New York: NYRB, 2001), p. xi.
25. *Lord of the Flies*, p. 65.
26. Ibid., p. 35.
27. Ibid., p. 67.
28. Ibid., p. 99.
29. Ibid., p. 140.
30. Ibid., p. 139.
31. Ibid. 45–46.
32. Ibid., p. 74.
33. Ibid., p. 76.

Notes to Freedom and Responsibility

1. See Michael Keren, *The Pen and the Sword: Israeli Intellectuals and the Making of the Nation-State* (Boulder, CO: Westview, 1989).
2. See Jacob Raz, *The Authority of Law: Essays on Law and Morality* (Oxford: Clarendon, 1979).
3. See Michael Walzer, *Obligations: Essays on Disobedience, War and Citizenship* (Cambridge, MA: Harvard University Press, 1970).
4. See Robert Jungk, *Brighter than a Thousand Suns: A Personal History of the Atomic Scientists* (New York: Harcourt Brace, 1958).
5. See Daniel Goldhagen, *Hitler's Willing Executioners: Ordinary Germans and the Holocaust* (New York: Knopf, 1996).
6. See Michael Ignatieff, *The Warrior's Honor: Ethnic War and the Modern Conscience* (New York: Viking, 1998.
7. Jean-Paul Sartre, *Existentialism and Humanism* (London: Methuen, 1948), p. 28.
8. Ibid., pp. 31–32.
9. Ibid., pp. 29–30.
10. Albert Camus, *The Outsider* (London: Penguin, 1983), p. 9.
11. Ibid.
12. Ibid., p. 22.
13. Ibid.
14. Ibid., p. 31.
15. Ibid.
16. Conor Cruise O'Brien, *Camus* (London: Fontana/Collins, 1970).
17. Patrick McCarthy, *Albert Camus the Stranger* (New York: Cambridge University Press, 1990).
18. *The Outsider*, p. 26.
19. Albert Camus, *The First Man* (Toronto: Knopf, 1994), pp. 279–80.
20. *The Outsider*, p. 57.
21. Ibid., p. 44.
22. Ibid., p. 49.
23. Ibid., p. 54.
24. Ibid., p. 58.
25. Ibid., p. 50.
26. Ibid., p. 56.
27. Ibid., p. 50.
28. Ibid., p. 58.

Notes to And History Continues

1. Elsa Morante, *History a Novel* (New York: Vintage, 1984), p. 37.
2. Ibid., p. 27.
3. Ibid., p. 3.
4. Ibid.
5. Ibid., p. 38.
6. Ibid., p. 407.
7. Ibid., p. 22.
8. Ibid., p. 35.

9   Ibid., p. 476.
10 Ibid., p. 489.
11 Ibid., p. 55.
12 Ibid.
13 Ibid., p. 56.
14 Ibid., p. 89.
15 Ibid., pp. 342–43.
16 Ibid., p. 13.
17 Ibid.
18 Ibid., p. 15.
19 Ibid., p. 61.
20 Ibid., p. 62.
21 Hanna Arendt, *Eichman in Jerusalem: A Report on the Banality of Evil* (New York: Viking Press, 1970).
22 See Krishan Kumar, *Utopia and Anti-Utopia in Modern Times* (Oxford: Basil Blackwell, 1991).
23 J.L. Talmon, *Political Messianism: The Romantic Phase* (London: Secker & Warburg, 1960).
24 *History A Novel*, p. 82.
25 Ibid., p. 143.
26 Ibid., p. 136.
27 Ibid., p. 317.
28 Ibid., p. 555.

Notes to Being There

1   See Herbert Marcuse, *One Dimensional Man: Studies in the Ideology of Advanced Industrial Society* (Boston: Beacon, 1964; C. Wright Mills, *The Power Elite* (New York: Oxford University Press, 1956); Marshall McLuhan, *Understanding Media: The Extensions of Man* (New York: McGraw Hill, 1964); Neil Postman, *Amusing Ourselves to Death: Public Discourse in the Age of Show Business* (New York: Penguin, 1985).
2   See Sandra Braman and Anabelle Steberny-Mohammadi, eds., *Globalization, Communication and Transnational Civil Society* (Cresskill, NJ: Hampton Press, 1998).
3   See David Paletz and Robert M. Entman, *Media, Power, Politics* (New York: Free Press, 1981).
4   Jerzy Kosinski, *Being There* (New York: Grove, 1970), p. 34.
5   Ibid., p. 14.
6   Ibid., p. 70.
7   Ibid., p. 139.
8   Ibid., p. 64–65.
9   Ibid., p. 54.
10 Ibid., p. 90.
11 Ibid., p. 40.
12 The description of Kosinski's life is based on James Park Sloan, *Jerzy Kosinski: A Biography* (New York: Dutton, 1996).
13 *Being There*, p. 36.
14 Ibid., p. 63.

15 On virtual reality and its implications, see Katheine N. Hayles, *How We Became Posthuman: Virtual Bodies in Cybernetics, Literature and Information* (Chicago: Chicago University Press, 1999).
16 See, for example, Neil Nevitte, *The Decline of Deference: Canadian Value Change in Cross-Cultural Perspective* (Peterborough, ON: Broadview, 1996); Max Kaase and Kenneth Newton, *Beliefs in Government* (New York: Oxford University Press, 1995).
17 *Being There*, p. 112.
18 Martin Buber, "Biblical Leadership." In *On the Bible: Eighteen Studies by Martin Buber*, Nahum N. Glatzer, ed. (New York: Schocken, 1968), p. 144.

Notes to Death of the Novel?

1 Allan Bloom, *Shakespeare's Politics* (New York: Basic Books, 1964), p. 2.
2 Ibid.
3 See Todd Kontje, *Private Lives in the Public Sphere: The German Bildungsroman as Metafiction* (University Park: Pennsylvania State University Press, 1992).
4 Martha C. Nussbaum, *Poetic Justice: The Literary Imagination and Public Life* (Boston: Beacon, 1995), p. 8.
5 See: Alvin Kernan, *The Death of Literature* (New Haven: Yale University Press, 1990), pp. 147–48.
6 Ibid., p. 151.
7 William Gamson, *Talking Politics* (Cambridge: Cambridge University Press, 1992).
8 See: Peter Lunt and Sonia M. Livingstone, *Talk on Television: Audience Participation and Public Debate* (London: Routledge, 1994).
9 See Denis McQuail and Karen Siune, *Media Policy: Convergence, Concentration and Commerce* (London: Sage, 1998).
10 Nancy Fraser, "Rethinking the Public Sphere: A Contribution to the Critique of Actually Existing Democracy." In *Habermas and the Public Sphere*, Craig Calhoun, ed. (Cambridge, MA: MIT Press, 1994), p. 110.
11 *The Structural Transformation of the Public Sphere*, pp. 50–51.
12 Ibid., p. 160.
13 Ibid., p. 172.
14 George Yúdice, "For a Practical Aesthetics." In *The Phantom Public Sphere*, pp. 218–19.
15 Ibid., p. 219.
16 Ibid.
17 Robert Detweiler, *Uncivil Rites: American Fiction, Religion, and the Public Sphere* (Urbana: University of Illinois, 1996), p. 4.
18 Ibid.
19 Nicolas Garnham, "The Media and the Public Sphere." In *Habermas and the Public Sphere*, Craig Calhoun, ed. (Cambridge, MA: MIT Press, 1994), pp. 369–70.
20 Ibid., pp. 374–75.
21 Wade Roland, *The Spirit of the Web: The Age of Information from Telegraph to Internet* (Toronto: Key Porter, 1999), p. 186.
22 Wilna A.J. Meijer, "Learning by Passion: The Literary Art Tradition and the Mass Media." *Interchange* 32/34 (2001): 339.
23 Robert Fulford, *The Triumph of Narrative: Storytelling in the Age of Mass Culture* (Toronto: Anansi, 1999).

Bibliography

Novels Analyzed in this Study
Camus, Albert. *The Outsider*, translated by Joseph Laredo. London: Penguin, 1983.
Golding, William. *Lord of the Flies*. New York: Capricon, 1959.
Huxley, Aldous. *Brave New World*. London: Granada, 1977.
Kafka, Franz. *The Trial*. New York: Schocken, 1992.
Kosinski, Jerzy. *Being There*. New York: Grove, 1970.
Mann, Thomas. *The Magic Mountain*, translated by H. T. Lowe-Porter. New York: Knopf, 1960.
Morante, Elsa. *History: A Novel*, translated by William Weaver. New York: Vintage Books, 1984.
Orwell, George. *1984*. New York: New American Library, 1961.

Other Works
Anderson, Benedict. *Imagined Communities: Reflections on the Origin and Spread of Nationalism*. London: Verso, 1991.
Baker, Gideon. "Problems in the Theoretisation of Global Civil Society." *Political Studies* 50 (2002): 928–43.
Baker, James R., ed. *Critical Essays on William Golding*. Boston: G. K. Hall, 1988.
Barber, Benjamin R. *Jihad vs. McWorld: How Globalism and Tribalism are Reshaping the World*. New York: Ballantine Books, 1996.
Barker, Robert S. *Brave New World: History, Science and Dystopia*. Boston: Twayne, 1990.
Beauchamp, Gorman. "Orwell, The Lysenko Affair and the Politics of Social Construction." *Partisan Review* 68 (2001): 266–79.
Bell, Michael. *Literature, Modernism and Myth: Belief and Responsibility in the Twentieth Century*. Cambridge: Cambridge University Press, 1997.
Bennett, Jane. "Deceptive Comfort: The Power of Kafka's Stories." *Political Theory* 19 (February 1991): 73–95.
———. "Kafka, Genealogy, and the Spiritualization of Politics." *The Journal of Politics* 56 (1994): 650–70.
Berube, Maurice R. *Beyond Modernism and Postmodernism: Essays on the Politics of Culture*. Westport, CT: Bergin & Garvey, 2002.
Bloom, Allan. *Shakespeare's Politics*. New York: Basic Books, 1964.
Bloom, Harold, ed. *The Western Canon: The Books and School of the Ages*. New York: Riverhead, 1994.
———. *Thomas Mann's The Magic Mountain*. New York: Chelsea, 1986.
Blotner, Joseph L. *The Political Novel*. Garden City, NY: Doubleday, 1955.
Braman, Sandra, and Anabelle Steberny-Mohammadi, eds. *Globalization, Communication and Transnational Civil Society*. Cresskill, NJ: Hampton Press, 1998.
Bronner, Stephen Eric. *Camus: Portrait of a Moralist*. Minneapolis: University of Minnesota Press, 1999.

Boulding, Kenneth E. *The Meaning of the Twentieth Century: The Great Transition*. New York: Harper & Row, 1964.

Cantor, Paul A. "Literature and Politics; Understanding the Regime." *PS: Political Science and Politics* 28 (June 1995): 192–95.

Calhoun, Craig, ed. *Habermas and the Public Sphere*. Cambridge, MA: MIT Press, 1994.

Cappela, Joseph N., *Spiral of Cynicism: The Press and the Public Good*. New York: Oxford University Press, 1997.

Cohen-Solal, Annie. "Camus, Sartre and the Algerian War." *Journal of European Studies* 28 (March–June 1998): 43–51.

Cohen, Jean L., and Andrew Arato. *Civil Society and Political Theory*. Cambridge, MA: MIT Press, 1992.

Colas, Dominique. *Civil Society and Fanaticism: Conjoined Histories*. Stanford: Stanford University Press, 1997.

Dahlgren, Peter, and Colin Sparks. *Communication and Citizenship: Journalism and the Public Sphere in the New Media Age*. London: Routledge, 1991.

Dahrendorf, Ralf. *Reflections on the Revolution in Europe*. London: Chatto & Windus, 1990.

Davis, Lennard J. *Resisting Novels: Ideology and Fiction*. New York: Methuen, 1987.

Davison, Ray. *Camus: The Challenge of Dostoevsky*. Exeter: University of Exeter Press, 1997.

Deery, June. *Aldous Huxley and the Mysticism of Science*. London: Macmillan, 1996.

Delanty, Gerard. *Citizenship in a Global Age: Society, Culture*, Politics. Buckingham: Open University Press, 2000.

Detweiler, Robert. *Uncivil Rites: American Fiction, Religion, and the Public Sphere*. Urbana: University of Illinois, 1996.

Dolan, Paul J. *Of War and War's Alarms: Fiction and Politics in the Modern World*. New York: The Free Press, 1976.

Firchow, Peter Edgerly. *The End of Utopia: A Study of Aldous Huxley's Brave New World*. London: Associated University Presses, 1984.

Fussell, Paul. *The Great War and Modern Memory*. Oxford; Oxford University Press, 1975.

Goldfarb, Jeffrey C. *Civility and Subversion: The Intellectual in Democratic Society*. Cambridge: Cambridge University Press, 1998.

Goldman, Harvey. *Max Weber and Thomas Mann: Calling and the Shaping of the Self*. Berkeley: University of California Press, 1988.

Gozzi, Raymond. *The Power of Metaphor in the Age of Electronic Media*. Cresskill, NJ: Hampton Press, 1999.

Habermas, Jürgen. *The Structural Transformation of the Public Sphere: An Inquiry into a Category of Bourgeois Society*. Cambridge, MA: MIT Press, 1994.

Hall, John A., ed. *Civil Society: Theory, History, Comparison*. Cambridge: Polity Press, 1995.

Hanna, Martha. *The Mobilization of Intellect: French Scholars and Writers during the Great War*. Cambridge, MA: Harvard University Press, 1996.

Harrington, Michael. *The Accidental Century*. New York: Macmillan, 1965.

Hayles, Katheine N. *How We Became Posthuman: Virtual Bodies in Cybernetics, Literature and Information*. Chicago: University of Chicago Press, 1999.

Hayman, Ronald. *K: A Biography of Kafka*. London: Weidenfeld and Nicolson, 1981.

Hitchens, Christopher. *Acknowledged Legislation: Writers in the Public Sphere*. London: Verso, 2000.

Holub, Robert C. *Jürgen Habermas: Critic in the Public Sphere*. London: Routledge, 1991.

Horton, John, and Andrea T. Baumeister, eds. *Literature and the Political Imagination.* London: Routledge, 1996.
Howe, Irving, ed. *1984 Revisited: Totalitarianism in Our Century.* New York: Harper & Row, 1983.
———. *Politics and the Novel.* New York: Horizon, 1957.
Ignatieff, Michael. *The Warrior's Honor: Ethnic War and the Modern Conscience.* New York: Viking, 1998.
Janoski, Thomas. *Citizenship and Civil Society: A Framework of Rights and Obligations in Liberal, Traditional, and Social Democratic Regimes.* Cambridge: Cambridge University Press, 1998.
Johnson, Paul. *A History of the Modern World: from 1917 to the 1980s.* London: Weidenfeld and Nicolson, 1983.
Keren, Michael. "The Civil Society and its Enemies: The Case of Israel." *Review of Constitutional Studies* 5 (1999): 33–52.
———. *The Pen and the Sword: Israeli Intellectuals and the Making of the Nation-State.* Boulder, CO: Westview, 1989.
Kernan, Alvin. *The Death of Literature.* New Haven, CT: Yale University Press, 1990.
Kingwell, Mark. *The World We Want: Virtue, Vice, and the Good Citizen.* Toronto: Penguin, 2000.
Klawitter, Uwe. *The Theme of Totalitarianism in 'English Fiction': Koestler, Orwell, Vonnegut, Kosinski, Burgess, Atwood, Amis.* Frankfurt: Peter Lang, 1997.
Kontje, Todd. *Private Lives in the Public Sphere: The German Bildungsroman as Metafiction.* University Park, PA: Pennsylvania State University Press, 1992.
Kumar, Krishan. *Utopia & Anti-utopia in Modern Times.* Oxford: Basil Blackwell, 1991.
Kundera, Milan, ed. *The Art of the Novel.* New York: Grove Press, 1988.
Lehring, Percy B. "Toward a Multicultural Civil Society: The Role of Social Capital and Democratic Citizenship." *Government and Opposition* 33 (Spring 1998): 221–42.
Lila, Mark. *The Reckless Mind: Intellectuals in Politics.* New York: NYRB, 2001.
McLuhan, Marshall. *The Gutenberg Galaxy: The Making of Topographic Man.* Toronto: University of Toronto Press, 1962.
———. *Understanding Media: The Extension of Man.* New York: Mentor, 1964.
McQuail, Denis, and Karen Siune. *Media Policy: Convergence, Concentration and Commerce.* London: Sage, 1998.
McCarthy, Mary. *Ideas and the Novel.* New York: Harcourt Brace Jovanovich, 1980.
McCarthy, Patrick. *Albert Camus the Stranger.* New York: Cambridge University Press, 1990.
Meijer, Wilna A. J. "Learning by Passion: The Literary Arts Tradition and the Mass Media." *Interchange* 32/4 (2001): 331–48.
Miller, Toby. *Technologies of Truth: Cultural Citizenship and the Popular Media.* Minneapolis: University of Minnesota Press, 1998.
Mulvihill, Robert, ed. *Reflections on America, 1984: An Orwell Symposium.* Athens, GA: University of Georgia Press, 1986.
Newsinger, John. *Orwell's Politics.* New York: St. Martin's Press, 1999.
Nussbaum, Martha C. *Poetic Justice: The Literary Imagination and Public Life.* Boston: Beacon, 1995.
O'Brien, Conor Cruise. *Camus.* London: Fontana/Collins, 1970.
Orwell, George. *Inside the Whale and Other Essays.* Harmondsworth: Penguin, 1957.

Paletz, David, and Robert M. Entman. *Media, Power, Politics.* New York: Free Press, 1981.

Postman, Neil. *Amusing Ourselves to Death: Public Discourse in the Age of Show Business.* New York: Penguin, 1985.

Price, Monroe E. *Television, The Public Sphere, and National Identity.* Oxford: Clarendon, 1995.

Putnam, Robert D. *Bowling Alone: The Collapse and Revival of American Community.* New York: Touchstone, 2000.

Rai, Alok. *Orwell and the Politics of Despair.* Cambridge: Cambridge University Press, 1988.

Reed, Walter L. *Meditations on the Hero: A Study of the Romantic Hero in Nineteenth-Century Fiction.* New Haven, CT: Yale University Press, 1974.

Reilly, Patrick. *The Literature of Guilt: From Gulliver to Golding.* Iowa City: University of Iowa Press, 1988.

Richetti, John. "The Novel and Society: The Case of Daniel Defoe." In *The Idea of the Novel in the Eighteenth Century,* Robert W. Uphaus, ed. East Lansing, MI: Colleagues Press, 1988.

Robbins, Bruce, ed. *The Phantom Public Sphere.* Minneapolis: University of Minnesota Press, 1993.

Rosenau, Pauline Marie. *Post-Modernism and the Social Sciences.* Princeton, NJ: Princeton University Press, 1992.

Savage, Robert L., James Combs, and Dan Nimmo, eds. *The Orwellian Moment: Hindsight and Foresight in the Post-1984 World.* Fayetteville: University of Arkansas Press, 1989.

Scharff, David E., ed. *The Psychoanalytic Century: Freud's Legacy for the Future.* New York: Other Press, 2001.

Seidman, Steven. *Contested Knowledge: Social Theory in the Postmodern Era.* Malden: Blackwell, 1998.

Sheldon, Michael. *Orwell: The Authorized Biography.* London: Heinemann, 1991.

Shoham, Shlomo Giora, and Francis Rosenstiel, eds. *And He Loved Big Brother: Man, State and Society in Question.* London: Macmillan, 1985.

Skinner, B.F. *Beyond Freedom and Dignity.* Toronto: Bantam, 1971.

Sloan, James Park. *Jerzy Kosinski: A Biography.* New York: Dutton, 1996.

Smith, Evans Lansing. *The Hero Journey in Literature: Parables of Poesis.* Lanham, MD: University Press of America, 1997.

Smith, Murray E.G., ed. *Early Modern Social Theory: Selected Interpretive Readings.* Toronto: Canadian Scholars' Press, 1998.

Sprintzen, David. *Camus: A Critical Examination.* Philadelphia: Temple University Press, 1988.

Steiner, George. "Our Homeland the Text." *Salmagundi* 66 (Winter–Spring 1985): 4–25.

Suchoff, David Bruce. *Critical Theory and the Novel: Mass Society and Cultural Criticism in Dickens, Melville, and Kafka.* Madison: University of Wisconsin Press, 1994.

Swift, Jamie. *Civil Society in Question.* Toronto: Between the Lines, 1999.

Tucker, Irene. *A Probable State: The Novel, the Contract, and the Jews.* Chicago: University of Chicago Press, 2000.

Talmon, J. L. *Political Messianism: The Romantic Phase.* New York: Praeger, 1960.

———. *The Origins of Totalitarian Democracy.* London: Secker and Warburg, 1952.

Tame, Peter D. *The Ideological Hero in the Novels of Robert Brasillach, Roger Vailland, and André Malraux.* New York: Peter Lang, 1998.

Tiger, Virginia. *William Golding: The Dark Fields of Discovery*. London: Calder and Boyars, 1974.

Urzidil, Johannes. *The Living Contribution of Jewish Prague to Modern German Literature*. New York: Leo Baeck Institute, 1968.

Varricchio, Mario. "Power of Images/Images of Power in Brave New World and Nineteen Eighty Four." *Utopian Studies* 10 (1999): 98–116.

Volti, Rudi. *Society and Technological Change*. New York: St. Martin's Press, 1995.

Walter, Hugo G. *Space and Time on the Magic Mountain: Studies in Nineteenth and Early Twentieth-Century European Literature*. New York: Peter Lang, 1999.

Walzer, Michael. *Obligations: Essays on Disobedience, War and Citizenship*. Cambridge, MA: Harvard University Press, 1970.

———. "The Civil Society Argument." In *Theorizing Citizenship*, Ronald Beiner, ed.. Albany: State University of New York Press, 1995.

Watts, Harold H. *Aldous Huxley*. New York: Twayne, 1969.

Windschuttle, Keith. *The Killing of History: How Literary Critics and Social Theorists are Murdering Our Past*. New York: The Free Press, 1996.

Woodcock, George. *Orwell's Message: 1984 and the Present*. Madeira Park, B.C.: Harbour, 1984.

Zuckert, Catherine. "Why Political Scientists Want to Study Literature." *PS: Political Science and Politics* 29 (1995): 189–90.

Index

Anarchism, 113–16
   defined, 114
Animal Farm (Orwell), 70
Arendt, Hannah, 69, 119
Aristotle, Aristotelian, 3, 131, 133
Arturo's Island (Morante), 110
Auden, W. H., 25
Authenticity, 10, 55, 59, 63, 68, 138
   defined, 57

The Balkanization of the West (Mestrovic), 84
Banality of evil, 119
Barber, Benjamin, 3–4
Barzun, Jacques, 21
Beauchamp, Gorman, 82
Baumeister, Andrea, 12
Being There (Kosinski), 2, 123, 128, 130, 133–34
Bennett, Jane, 40
"Big Brother", 2, 69, 73, 77, 87, 142
Bill of Rights, 62

Bismarck, Otto von, 35
Blair, Tony, 123
Bloom, Allan, 137–38
Boulding, Kenneth, 55
"Brave New World", 2, 8, 58–64
Brave New World (Huxley), 1, 56–59, 62, 64–65
Brod, Max, 39
Brecht, Bertolt, 6
Buber, Martin, 134–35
Bureaucracy, bureaucracies, 8, 35–38, 41–47, 49, 51, 95, 138, 142
Bureaucratic, 100, 125
   apparatus, 37, 39, 44
   authority structure, 36
   institutions, 121, 130
   life, 36
   maneuvering, 142
   model, 45
   monsters, 9
   nightmares, 51
   organization, 45

routines, 47
state, 38
structures, 37–38, 42, 48, 142
wheel, 48
world, 49
Bureaucrats, 4–5, 37, 76
Bureaucratization, 2

Caligula (Camus), 102
Camus, Albert, 1, 8–9, 102–8
Cantor, Paul, 7–8
Chaplin, Charlie, 56
Chauncey Gardiner, 1, 8, 10, 125–35, 138, 149
"Chemical Persuasion" (Huxley), 62
Christ, 26
Citizens, 3–5, 9–11, 13, 56, 72–75, 111, 131, 138–39, 142
  and civil society, 2–3
  and commitment to the state, 100
  and natural rights, 57
  and obligation, 11
  and overflow of information, 72
  and public voice, 4–5
  and responsibility, 100–101, 108
  and state control, 57
  idealized, 141
  vs. sovereign individual, 4
Citizenship, 3–4, 31, 71, 139–40
  global, 143
Civil, civic (*see also* civil society, civility)
  activity, 3
  consciousness, 6
  education, 74
  identity, 4
  message, 149
  opposition, 6
  organizations, 53
  service, 36
Civil society, 2–5, 7, 64, 89, 143 (*see also* civil, civic, civility)
  and bureaucracy, 47
  and civility, 9

and democracy, 3
and the media, 4
defined, 2
global, 2–3
model of, 10, 137–38
theorists, 138
uses of the term, 3
Civility, 13, 53, 68, 71, 76, 87, 97–98, 142, 147, 149 (*see also* civil, civic, civil society)
  defined, 9
Civility and Subversion (Goldfarb), 6
Civilized, 75, 86
  community, 90
  constitutional regimes, 3
  humanity, 22
  life, 59
CNN, 72
Comba, 102
Communism, Communist, 5, 6, 23, 60, 95, 100, 102, 111, 113, 131
Comte, Auguste, 20
Conrad, Joseph, 20
Convergence, 142
Cooper, Thomas, 77
Cover-up culture, 66
Crick, Francis, 25
Cronkite, Walter, 77

Dante, 28, 137
Darwinian, 2, 24
De Kerckhove, Derrick, 147
The Death of Literature (Kernan), 140
Democracy, democracies, 3, 30, 37, 56, 70–72, 74, 90, 95, 97, 145
  and viability, 124
  mass, 35
  of procedure, 97
  true, 129
  Western, 67
Democratic, democratization, 49, 69–71, 73–77, 93, 95, 97, 100, 123, 128, 141
Detweiler, Robert, 145

Dolan, Paul, 12,
Dostoevsky, Fyodor, 29, 101
Dr. Jekyll and Mr. Hyde (Stevenson), 57
Drucker, Peter, 51
Durkheim, Émile, 21
Dylan, Bob, 25

"Education after the Culture Wars" (Ravitch), 82
Eichmann, Adolph, 119
Einstein, Albert, 15–16, 25
Eliot, T. S., 25
Ellul, Jacques, 55–56
Existentialism, 101
Ezekiel, 120

Failures, 131, 133–35
Fascism, fascists, 5, 16, 23, 57, 59, 63, 85–86, 93, 95–97, 111, 113–14, 116–17
Faustian pact, 59
Fernandel, 103
The First Man (Camus), 102, 104–6
Flaubert, Gustave, 7
The Forty Days of Musa Dagh (Werfel), 39
Frankenstein (Shelley), 57
Freedom of expression, 71
Freud, Sigmund, Freudian, 15–16, 24–25, 59, 89
Friedrich, Carl, 69
Fulford, Robert, 148
Future Shock (Toffler), 56

Galbraith, John Kenneth, 5, 50, 55–56
Gamson, William, 141
Gandhi, Mahatma, 114
Garnham, Nicholas, 145–46
Geertz, Clifford, 148
Globalization, 5, 67
Goethe, Johann Wolfgang von, 137
Goldfarb, Jeffry, 6

Golding, William, 1, 8–9, 89–92, 94–97
Grant, Cary, 126

Habermas, Jürgen, 143–45
Hanna, Martha, 32
Hans Castorp, 1, 8, 10, 18–20, 22–23, 25–28, 33, 138, 147, 149
Harrington, Michael, 16
Hayman, Ronald, 38
Hegel, Georg Wilhelm Friedrich, 3, 7, 19
Heidegger, Martin, 95
History (Morante), 2, 109–11, 120–22
Hitchens, Christopher, 6,
Hitler, Adolf, 17, 25, 38, 71, 85, 109–10, 112
Hobbes, Thomas, 90
Holocaust, 5, 99
Homage to Catalonia (Orwell), 85
Homer, 11, 137
Horton, John, 12
House of Liars (Morante), 110
Howe, Irving, 7
Human rights, 4, 52, 71, 83–84 (*see also* rights of man)
Hussein, Saddam, 72
Huxley, Aldous, 1, 8, 56–59, 61–62, 64–67

Iacocca, Lee, 5
IBM, 52
Ida Ramundo, Ida, 1, 8, 10, 110–14, 117–19, 121–22, 138, 149
Ideological, ideology, ideologies, 2, 5, 8–9, 21, 23
Ideology and Utopia (Mannheim), 23
Internet, 1, 25, 77–79, 139–41
addiction, 79

Jihad vs. McWorld (Barber), 3
John the Savage, 1, 8, 10, 57–59, 64, 138, 149
Johnson, Lyndon Baines (LBJ), 129
Johnson, Paul, 15
The Joke (Kundera), 6
Joseph K., K., 1, 8, 10, 38–39, 41–50, 52–53, 138, 149

Kabbalah, 40
Kafka, Franz, Kafkaean, 1, 8–9, 38–41, 49–53, 65, 74, 142
Kantian humanism, 70
Kennedy, John Fitzgerald, 25
Kennedy, Ted, 126
Kernan, Alvin, 140
Kierkegaard, Soren, 101
The Killing of History (Windschuttle), 80
King David, 135
Kingwell, Mark, 4, 9
Knowledge elites, 50
Kosinski, Jerzy, 2, 8–9, 123–25, 128–34
Krylov's fables, Krylovian, 128–29
Kropotkin, Peter, 114
Kundera, Milan, 6–7, 148

Lenin, Vladimir Illich, 5, 25, 38
Lepsius, Johannes, 39
Lewinkopf, Mojzesz, 130
Liberalism, 65
Lilla, Mark, 95
Locke, John, 90
"Looking Back on the Spanish War" (Orwell), 86
Lord of the Flies (Golding), 1, 89–90, 96
Lukács, Georg, 17

Machiavelli, Niccolo, 39
MacIntyre, Alasdair, 148
The Magic Mountain (Th. Mann), 1, 16–18, 20, 25, 27, 31, 33, 40
Management, 37, 51–52, 65
Managers, 5, 37, 51, 66
Managerial revolution, 51
Mann, Heinrich, 17, 29
Mann, Katia, 17
Mann, Thomas, 1, 8, 16–17, 19, 24, 32–33, 40, 147
Mannheim, Karl, 21, 23
Marcuse, Herbert, 133
Marx, Marxism, Marxist, 15–17, 31, 119–20
Mazzini, Guissepe, 29
McCarthy era, 17
McLuhan, Marshall, 133
The Meaning of the Twentieth Century (Boulding), 55
Media, mass media, 4–5, 52–53, 76–78, 84–85, 123–24, 127, 133–34, 138–44, 146–49
"Media Fascism", 77
Meijer, Wilna, 148
Memory, 81, 84–85, 87, 138
  historical, 10, 76, 79, 84–85, 87
Mendus, Susan, 12
Messiah, 39, 89, 120–22, 138
Messianic, 119, 122, 138 (*see also* political messianism)
  age, 120
  future, 6
  movements, 120
  politics, 149
  promise, 149
  rhetoric, 39, 113, 120
  yearnings, 9
  visions, 100
Mestrovic, Stjepan, 84
Meursault, 1, 8, 10, 102–3, 105–8, 138, 149
Microsoft, 52
Miller, Henry, 85
Modern industrial states, new industrial state, 2, 5, 23, 50–51, 56, 59, 63–66, 68, 111, 138

Modern Times (Chaplin), 56
Modernity, 35, 69
Molière, Jean-Baptiste Poquelin, 137
Morante, Elsa, 1–2, 8–9, 109–11, 113, 117, 119
Moravia, Alberto, 110
Moses, 135
Mussolini, Benito, Duce, 109–10, 112, 121–22
The Myth of Sisyphus (Camus), 102–3

Nasdaq, 51
Nations, 39, 72
Nation-state, 2, 39, 149
　defined, 99
Nationalism, national movements, 38–39
　and political messianism, 120
　liberal, 29
Nationalists, nationalistic, 32, 39, 112
Nazism, Nazi, 9, 69, 95, 100, 110, 112–13, 117–19, 129
1984 (Orwell), 1, 69–71, 73, 75–79, 81, 142
The New Industrial State (Galbraith), 50, 55
New York Times, 128, 130
Nietzschean, 18
Novelists, writers, authors, 1, 5, 7–8, 23–24, 137, 145
　and the collapse of totalitarianism, 6
Nurenberg trials, 100
Nussbaum, Martha, 138

O'Brien, Connor Cruise, 104
One Day in the Life of Ivan Denisovich (Solzhenitzyn), 6
The Open Society and its Enemies (Popper), 120
Organizations, organizational, 2, 8, 36–38, 40–42, 44–53, 66, 93–94, 138, 149
The Organization Man (Whyte), 49
Orwell, George (Blaire, Arthur Eric), 1, 8–9, 69–71, 74, 76–82, 85–87, 142

Orwellian, 76, 78–79

Pacifism, 114
The Painted Bird (Kosinski), 129
Pascalian bet, wager, 145–46
Pasha, Enver, 39
The Passion of the Western Mind (Tarnas), 23
Picasso, Pablo, 25
The Plague (Camus), 102
Plato, Platonic, 11, 120
Poetic Justice (Nussbaum), 138–39
Political correctness, 82
"Political man", 42
Political messianism, 120
Political novel, 7, 109
Popper, Karl, 120
Post-modern, post-modernism, post-modernist, 79–81, 84
Postman, Neil, 133
Powell, Colin, 128
Prague Circle, 38–39
Press, 29, 59, 61, 133
Psychoanalysis, 20, 23–26

Rabin, Yitzhak, 106
Racine, Jean Baptiste, 137
Ralph, 1, 8, 10, 90–92, 94, 96–98, 138, 149
Ravitch, Diane, 82
Reagan, Ronald, 66, 123
Reason, 10–11, 19–21, 80, 82–83, 89–92, 95–96, 98, 138
　community of, 97
Reasoning, 20, 139
The Reckless Mind (Lilla), 95
Redemption, redeeming, 10, 30, 33, 39–40, 90, 120–22, 138
Republic (Plato), 11
Responsibility, 10, 99–102, 108
　and freedom, 108
　legal, 100

Reubeni Fürst der Juden (Brod), 39
Rights of man, 31 (*see also* human rights)
Roosevelt, Franklin, 25
Rosenau, Pauline Marie, 79
Rousseau, 29–30, 58, 80, 119, 128, 130
Rowland, Wade, 67, 147
Rule of law, 42, 71

Sadat, Anwar, 106
Salvation, 30
Sartre, Jean-Paul, 101–2
Schorske, Carl, 24
Science, 7, 9, 20–21, 27, 29–30, 57, 65, 138 (*see also* social sciences, social scientists)
Scientific, 7–8, 10, 18–19, 26, 58, 61, 65, 99, 111, 129
   revolution, 119
Scientists, 5, 12, 21, 56, 76
   and responsibility, 100
Schmidt, Carl, 95
Shakespeare's Politics (Bloom), 137
Shakesperean, 137, 141
"Shooting an Elephant" (Orwell), 70
Social contracts, 21, 57, 90
Social sciences, social scientists, 20–22, 80 (*see also* science)
Sociologists, 12, 20–21, 37, 76
Sociology, 23
   ambitions, promise of, 22
   of knowledge, 23
   origins of, 20
Socrates, Socratic, 51, 92
Solidarity movement, 3
Solzhenitzyn, Alexander, 6
Spanish Civil War, 85
Springer, Jerry, 4
St. Augustine, Augustinian, 119–20, 122
Stalin, Stalinist, 69, 71, 74, 85, 100, 109–10, 117

Steiner, George, 40
The Stranger (Camus), 1, 102–4, 106
Stravinsky, Igor, 25
Stromberg, Ronald, 32
The Structural Transformation of the Public Sphere (Habermas), 143
Swift, Jonathan, 22
Swingewood, Alan, 20

Talmon, Jacob, 69, 120
Tarnas, Richard, 23–24
Taylor, Frederick Winslow, 5
Technological, 2, 8, 60, 68, 72, 76, 99
   age, 29, 62
   civilization, 58–59
   development, 64
   devil, 58
   project, 62, 66
   revolution, 51, 56–58
   society, 64
   solutions, 59
   supremacy, 67
   transition, 55
   world, 59
The Technological Society (Ellul), 55
Technology, technologies, 5, 7–8, 27–29, 55–56, 58–60, 63, 65, 67, 76, 83, 138, 149
   American, 66
   and choice, 29
   and hedonism, 62
   and loss of authenticity, 59
   and democracy, 59, 77
   defined, 56
   fear of, 57
   medical, 27
Technocracy, technocratic class, elite, "technostructure", 50, 56, 76
Technocrats, 76–77
Thrasymachus, 11, 46
Tiger, Virginia, 89
Toffler, Alvin, 56
Tolstoy, Lev Nikolayevich, 114
Totalitarian, 61, 69–72, 75, 78, 131

states, 40, 42, 128
Totalitarianism, 6, 39, 70–71, 73–74, 95, 131
  defined, 69
The Trial (Kafka), 1, 38–41, 46–47, 50, 52, 142
Tropic of Cancer (Miller), 85
The Triumph of Narrative (Fulford), 148
Truth and Reconciliation Commission, 83
Tse-tung, Mao, 112
Tutu, Desmond, 83
Tuchman, Barbara, 66
Turner, Mark, 149

Utopianism, 119

Village Voice, 130
Virtual, 139
  activities, 127
  images, 132, 140
  order, 133
  politics, 9, 127, 132
  reality, 1, 124, 132–33
  world, 132
Voltaire, Voltairean, 20, 22, 30

Walzer, Michael, 3
Watson, James, 25
Weber, Max, Weberian, 5, 21, 35–37, 45
Werfel, Franz, 39
Whyte, William, 49–50, 52
Wilson, James Q., 81
Windschuttle, Keith, 80
Winston Smith, 1, 8, 10, 70–73, 75, 77–79, 81, 87, 138, 149
The World We Want (Kingwell), 4

Yúdice, George, 144–45

Zionism, 39, 113
Zuckert, Catherine, 13
Zweig, Stephan, 16